# GOPESHWAR

## Mirror of the Art of Uttarakhand (Himalaya)

# *GOPESHWAR*

## *Mirror of the Art of Uttarakhand (Himalaya)*

**D.N. Dimri**

*Foreword by*

**Dr. B.R. Mani**
**Additional Director General**
**A.S.I. New Delhi**

**Kaveri Books**
New Delhi-110002

First Published in 2012
ISBN 978-81-7479-131-3



*Published by*
**Kaveri Books**
4832/24, Ansari Road
New Delhi - 110 002 (India)
Tel.: 011-2328 8140, 2324 5799,
Fax: 011-2328 8140
E-mail: kaveribooks@vsnl.com,
kaveribooks@gmail.com
Website: www.kaveribooks.com

*Laser Typesetting by :* Deep Graphics, Delhi

*Printed at :* Salasar Imaging Systems, Delhi-110 052

PRINTED IN INDIA

*Dedicated*

*to*

*My Parents*

# FOREWORD

It gives us pleasure to have this handy book on Gopeshwar which the author and my colleague in ASI Sri D.N. Dimri has written with utmost clarity, accuracy and scholarship.

The group of temples at Gopeshwar and the local tradition attracts attention of everyone who comes across the presiding deity Gopeshwar — Lord Shiva, the procession of yatra from Gopeshwar to Rudranath and back, the cluster of subsidiary shrines showing evolution of temple architecture, the double storeyed residential buildings - Tibari and Rawal Niwas, the inscribed shaft of the iron trident which is a metallurgical marvel of Ancient India in the style of one established by the Nāga rulers in about fourth century AD at Sudh-Mahadeva, near Udhampur (J&K state), the stone and metallic sculptures of various Brahmanical deities – some of which having excellent craftsmanship and artistic forms. A Brief account of such significant features is available in this book which I am sure would be a priced possession for a person who is interested in these monumental remains and heritage of our glorious past as preserved in Uttarakhand.

23rd March, 2012

**B.R.Mani**
Additional Director General,
Archaeological Survey of India,
Janpath, New Delhi - 110 001

# *PREFACE*

Gopeshwar, a sleepy town nestled in the Chamoli hills of Uttarakhand, was brought to scholarly attention by James Prinsep in 1836. He deciphered and published an inscription on the iron trident at Gopeshwar, eye copy of which was sent to the Asiatic Society, Kolkatta, by Traill. This inscription was further studied by Pandit Bhagwanlal Indraji who made some necessary amendments in Prinsep's reading and published his observations in *The Indian Antiquary: A Journal of Oriental Research*, VOL. X 1881. In the same year Edwin T. Atkinson visited Gopeshwar and described the religious importance of this place in his pioneer work, *The Himalayan Gazetteer*. In addition to what Prinsep described, Atkinson also made reference to the temple of Mahādeva here. However, Gopeshwar remained in oblivion for about a century till K.P. Nautiyal published his research work in 1969. A huge credit goes to Nautiyal for conducting a systematic archaeological investigation of the Central Himalayan region for the first time. His work is still considered as a reference point by the present scholars. While describing the salient features of Central Himalayan art, Nautiyal also made references to some select sculptures housed in the Śiva temple at Gopeshwar. In the subsequent years, Yaswant Singh Katoch conducted an extensive survey of this area and wrote about the trident inscriptions of Gopeshwar while discussing art and architecture of the Central Himalayan region as a whole. He also described a few sculptures from Gopeshwar in his works. In the year 1994, B.M. Khanduri of HNB University, Srinagar, Garhwal, published his work wherein he dealt with different aspects of archaeology of the region under reference and also described some of the important images of Gopeshwar. Other scholars also conducted researches on various disciplines of archaeology of this region but a comprehensive study on art seems to have remained neglected.

The first ever critical study on the art of Central Himalaya was carried out by M.P. Joshi of Kumaun University (1989). He suggested that the art of Central Himalaya should be christened "Katyūrī Art". He not only explained the salient features of the Katyūrī Art but also discussed the stages of its genesis, florescence and decadence, which synchronise with the rise and fall of the Katyūrī dynasty.

While preparing an inventory of the sculptures at Gopeshwar, some hitherto unnoticed interesting sculptures were found. Significantly, these sculptures, made in local course-grained stone, leave no room for doubt that the genesis of the Katyūrī art took place in the Central Himalayan region itself, and Gopeshwar is one such place where the different phases of the Katyūrī art are clearly noticeable; thus the site serves as a mirror of Central Himalayan art. Here, art activities in the form of stone carvings seem to have taken place sometime from the sixth century AD. In its initial stage it was inspired by the Gupta art traditions of Central India, and subsequently it developed its own style and reached its peak during the 9th and 10th centuries AD, when the entire Central Himalayan region was under the sway of the Katyūrī rulers. From 12th century onwards the Katyūrī kingdom began to decline, the implications of which are also reflected on the art activities of Gopeshwar.

I do not claim to be an expert in Indian art. Nevertheless, while verifying these images I felt that this handbook will definitely serve as a beginner's guide to students, scholars and uninitiated readers who want to study the art of Uttarakhand Himalaya. I am grateful to Prof. M.P. Joshi who has generously helped in iconographic interpretation of the sculptors at the site, revising and editing the drafts of the manuscript and helping me in every way possible during my research.

I am extremely thankful to Sh. C. Dorji, Jt. Director General, Archaeological Survey of India who inspire me and remain instrumental behind publication of this small monograph.

I would like to thank Neeraj Kumar Verma, Assistant Archaeologist of Dehradun Circle, for providing necessary help while preparing the manuscript. Many thanks to Devdhar Dubey, Surveyor, for preparing the line-drawings of the temple. I would also like to thank Mohamad Yasin and Shri Sushil Yadav for typing the text.

Last but not the least I would like to thank my wife Kamla and my children Manish and Mohini and daughter-in-law Shikha without whom it was not possible to complete this task.

**D.N. Dimri**

## *CONTENTS*

# 1

## *INTRODUCTION*

Gopeshwar, the headquarters of District Chamoli, is situated between 30° 28' 8"N and 79° 16' 15" E in the state of Uttarakhand (Pls. 1&2). It is well connected with motorable road from Rishikesh in Garhwal and from Haldwani/Nainital/Almora in Kumaon region. From Chamoli, located on the Rishikesh-Badrinath National Highway, one has to cross the Alaknanda river and travel about ten kms of hilly terrain to reach this holy place. From Gopehswar the same road further leads to Gourikund via Ukhimath, Guptkashi and Gaurikund, thence the famous Kedarnath shrine is about fourteen km on the walkable track. Being located in the middle of the holy shrines of Kedarnath and Badrinath, Gopeshwar enjoys the reputation of being a halting point of pilgrimage from time immemorial.

The Śiva temple of Gopeshwar stands in the midst of the village of the same name (Pl.3). A large number of architectural members including *āmalakas* of various sizes suggest that originally the temple site was located in a vast area outside the enclosed boundary wall of the present temple complex (Pl.4).

Originally the temple owned a large area of land in its vicinity, wherein probably some of the ancient temples were constructed, remains of which in the form of architectural members, particularly the *āmalakas*, are still found in the temple complex itself. However, in course of time, when the British introduced permanent land ownership to earn revenue from individual owners, the land surrounding the temple under reference was settled in the names of individual proprietors. It accounts for the construction of private residential buildings around the present temple complex.

In addition to main temple there are three miniature shrines within the temple complex locally known as Mātā Mandir, Gaṇeśa and Navadurgā temples. Except Mātā Mandir which still preserves its original architectural features, the other shrines have lost their originality due to modifications in the later periods (Pls.5 -6).

There are two double-storied buildings made in the traditional style of the Central Himalayan residential architectural within the premises. The one on the right behind the main temple is called *Tibārī* (*baradari*) and the other known as Rāwal Niwās. The latter is situated on the back of the main temple. The upper floor of *baradari* houses a metal image of Mālū Devata riding a bull. Mālū appears to be a folk form of Śiva worshiped by the local people. However, it is not known when this practice started. Traditionally, every year on the full moon day of Margasirsh as per Hindu calendar the deity is taken out in a procession for a holy bath to Vaitarani (a water spring cum reservoir) situated about one kilometer away towards south-west of the main temple. Here a cluster of seven small shrines is found, one of which is constructed in *valabhi* style, and the remaining ones in the *latina* style. Stylistically, the *valabhi* shrine may be dated to *circa* tenth century AD. Close to it towards north-west is a *latina* shrine with *pañcharatha* plan (Pls. 6&7). To the best of our knowledge it is the only surviving *pañcharatha* shrine in Garhwal. Stylistically it may be dated to late twelfth or early thirteenth century AD. The remaining shrines are highly stylized and may have been constructed between fourteenth and seventeenth centuries AD. Some of the rituals which take place in the main temple are supplemented here.

Rāwal Niwās, another important double-storied building with open courtyard within the shrine complex, was meant for the residence of Rāwal, chief priest of the temple who hails from South India (Pl.8). Tradition holds that originally the temple of Gopeshwar was under the control of Kedarpitha and was worshipped by Jangam Gusāīṁ Viraśaiva sect of South India. This practice prevailed here till recent times, but due to some dispute among the Rāwal and the local residents the former lost his ritual status, and now local Brahmins are the priests of the temple. It may be noted here that the tradition of Rāwal as the chief priest from south still prevails at Badrinath and Kedarnath.

According to a popular tradition, the form in which Lord Śiva is worshipped at Gopeshwar also receives adoration at Rudranāth, located about 20 kms from Gopeshwar in remote Himalaya. Every year, on the day of *Sakranti* of *Jeshthamasa*, mostly falling in the last week of May or in the first week of June, Lord Śiva's metal image, placed on a wooden palanquin (*doli*), is taken to Rudranāth in a procession, where it is worshipped for six months in natural cave where Lord Śiva in the form of *mukhalingam* is already enshrined. During this period Śiva is worshiped both in Gopeshwar and Rudranāth. After six months during the winter season, the God returns to Gopeshwar in the same way as at the time of his departure. It is not known how and when this tradition started since the *Kedārakhaṇḍa*, the local *purāṇa*, is silent about this journey of Lord Śiva from Gopeshwar to Rudranāth. However, the presence of a few sculptures and votive temples at Rudranāth suggests that this tradition may have been fairly old. Stylistically, the temples at Rudranāth are of *prāggrīva* type and highly stylized, the earliest of which cannot be placed before the 12th century AD (Pl.9).

# 2

## *HISTORICAL BACKGROUND*

In popular belief the Himalayan ranges of Uttarakhand are held as Deva-bhumi, the land of gods. The presence of innumerable temple sites all over this newly-formed state vindicates this belief. However, human activity in this region dates back to the prehistoric times as evidenced from the discovery of painted rock shelters discovered at Gwrakhya Wadyar and Kimni (Nautiyal and Khanduri 1986; Saklani 1983). The discovery of some early burials at Malari (Chamoli) where a complete intact skeleton of a Jhabu (Himalyan yak), pottery, and a tiny gold mask were found in a grave, have been placed in the second-first millennium BC (Bhatt et. al. 2009).

Unfortunately, we have no archaeological records for the subsequent ages of local history till the advent of the Kunindas who held sway in Uttarakhand from at least second century BC to third century AD (see for details, Joshi 1989b). The most celebrated ruler of Uttarakhand was Poṇa Śīlavarman, who performed four *aśvamedha yajñas* as we learn from the Jagatgram Aśvamedha brick altar inscriptions dated to the last quarter of the third century AD (*IAR 1953-54*: 11-12;

Ramachandran 1955). Śīlavarman seems to have amalgamated different chiefdoms of Kuṇindas, and paved way for the rise of the monarchical kingdom of Karttṛipura that acknowledged the suzerainty of the Gupta emperor Samudragupta (*circa* AD 335-375) referred to in the *Prayāga Praśasti*, Allahabad (see for details, Joshi 1989b: 101-102; 2007). Karttṛipura has been identified with Kārttikeyapura (modern Baijnath, Bageshwar) of the Katyūrī inscriptions (Oldham 1898: 98; Sircar 1986: 258; Nautiyal 1969: 29). According to local traditions Joshimath (Chamoli) was the earliest capital of the Katyūrīs. It is assumed that "the possessions of these Joshimath Katyūrī extended from the Sutlej as far as the Gandaki and from the snow-clad hills to the plains including the whole of Rohilkhand" (Atkinson 1884: 467). Apparently, during the Gupta period the capital of the Katyūrīs was situated at Joshimath. The Pandukeshwar (Chamoli) copper plates of the Katyūrīs issued from Kārttikeyapura clearly show that Joshimath region was patronized by all branches of the Katyūrī dynasty. These copper plates have been dated between ninth and tenth centuries AD on the basis of internal evidence of the inscriptions and palaeography (see for details, Kielhorn 1896; Sircar 1955-56). Interestingly, some scholars (Dabral 2026 vs: Kathoch 1981: 149 ff) identified Kārttikeyapura with Joshimath itself. It was the Joshimath branch of the Katyūrīs that patronized art and architectural activities at Gopeshwar. Atkinson has given a detailed account of the transfer of Katyūrī capital from Joshimath to Katyur:

> "A descendant of Basdeo went on hunt in the jungles one day, and during his absence Vishnu, in his man-lion incarnation as Nar-Simha, taking the shape of a man, visited the place and asked the wife of the absent prince for food. The Rani gave

> the man enough to eat and after eating he lay down on the Raja's bed. When the raja returned from the chase and found a stranger asleep on his bed, he drew his sword and struck him on the arm, but instead of blood, milk flowed forth from the wound. The Raja was terrified at the omen and called his Rani to counsel and she said, "No doubt this is a devta: why did you strike him?' The Raja then addressed Nar-Simha and asked that his crime might be punished. On this the deity disclosed himself and said, 'I am Nar-Simha. I was pleased with thee and therefore came to thy darbar: now thy fault shall be punished in this wise: thou shalt leave this pleasant Jyotirtham and go into Katyur and there establish thy home. Remember that this wound which thou hast given me shall also be seen on the image in my temple, and when that image shall fall to pieces and the hand shall no more remain, thy house shall fall to ruin and thy dynasty shall disappear from amongst the princes of the world. (Atkinson Vol.-I PP 467-468)".

In fact, before the introduction of automobile in the Kedaranath-Badrinath pilgrimage, Gopeshwar served as one of the major halting religious centres of the pilgrimage under reference. According to local traditions the Kedaranath-Badrinath pilgrimage should be undertaken from Kedaranath, thence Gopeshwar, followed by Joshimath, Pandukeshwar, and finally Badrinath. It is likely that the early Katyūrīs played a key ritual role in facilitating this pilgrimage. It still continues to be discharged by the surviving descendants of the Garhwal ruling dynasty.

It may be noted here that scholars are of the opinion that the famous Katyūrī dynasty of Uttarakhand lineally descended from the Kuṇindas (Powell Price 1930; Joshi 2007). Tradition and archaeology indicate that from *circa* ninth to eleventh centuries AD the Katyūrī dynasty ruled over a vast region extending from Garhwal in the west to Doti (western Nepal) in the east. Inscriptions reveal that this region was occupied by the Mallas of Dullu (western Nepal). It resulted in the liquidation of the early Katyūrī kingdom, and emergence of several petty principalities within their territories. Eventually, there arose three major chieftaincies under the Raikā, Chandra, and Paṁvara dynasties, respectively in Doti (far-western Nepal), Kumaon, and Garhwal (see for details and references, Joshi 2005; 2009a). Archaeological remains show that throughout this period Gopeshwar continued to receive royal patronage.

Gopeshwar cannot be studied in isolation, for it forms an integral part of the cultural tradition of Uttarakhand in general and Garhwal Himalaya in particular. From the very early times this Himalayan region has been consecrated as the source of the most sacred rivers of India, namely, the Ganga and the Jamuna, and the great shrines of "Badari and Kedar, containing forms of Vishnu and Śiva which still hold a foremost position in the beliefs of the great majority of Hindus. To them the Kumaon Himalayas is what Palestine is to Christian... 'the great way' to final liberation" (Atkinson 1884: 703). Naturally, therefore, from very early times people from different parts of the country came on pilgrimage to this area, as is clear from several votive inscriptions, datable between second and seventh century AD, notably, the Devaprayag Brahmi inscriptions (Chhabra 1953-54), the Lakhamandal (Dehradun) stone slab inscription of Chhagaleśa (Chhabra 1944: 80-83), the Lakhamandal Praśasti of Īsvarā (Buhler 1892: 10-15), Palethi stone slab inscription of Kalyāṇavarman (Ram 1950: 273-77), the Siroli stone inscription of Naravarman, and the Barahat (Uttarkashi) trident inscription of Guha (*ARIE 1968-69*: 58). Chandikhal (Mahad) inscription of Vishṇuvarmmā (*IAR- 2010-11*: in press), and Taleshwar copper plate of Paurava-Varmans.

In Gopeshwar itself we find a colossal iron trident measuring over 5m high with a diameter of 20cm. Inscribed in late Brāhmī characters of sixth-seventh century AD it records its erection in front of the temple of Rudra by one Gaṇapatināga (*ARIE 1966-67*: 45) (Pl. 11&12). Interestingly, in course of time this trident seems to have fallen down and it was restored to its present position by King Aśoka Challa of Dulu, western Nepal, as we learn from his inscription on the same trident engraved in Nāgārī characters (Pl. 13). He also refers to a dated stone slab inscription from Gopeshwar recording *Saka* 1113 (AD 1191) issued by Aneka Malla. Recent studies have shown that Atkinson's reading is erroneous and that the correct reading is Asoka Challa (*ARIE 1966-67*: 45; see for details, Joshi 2009b). There are several other inscriptions found at Gopeshwar in eleventh-twelfth century Nāgārī characters recording names of chiefs (*ARIE 1966-67*: 43-45; Joshi 2011). According to Joshi (2010) the names ending in "Gusāīṁ" in these inscriptions represent the junior Katyūrīs whose descendants still bear the surname Gusāīṁ. Thus, we notice that at least from sixth to twelfth centuries AD Gopeshwar continually received royal patronage.

The iron trident of Gopeshwar bespeaks of the advance state of forger's skill and metallurgy. A somewhat similar but much larger trident of approximately the same period was set up by Guha (probably a king) at Uttarkashi. Use of metal in such non-utilitarian purpose shows easy availability of this material in this area. Setting up of such colossal tridents in a remote area in those days must have aroused the curiosity of the local people and inspired them to visit these sites which, in course of time, became established places of pilgrimage. These activities obviously influenced the social, economic and cultural life of the people of this hilly region. Interestingly, the locals have invented an interesting tradition about the iron trident. They ascribe it to lord Śiva believing that the site of the trident marks the place where Śiva was practicing austerity, and Kamadeva, the God of Love, tried to interrupt it by shooting arrows of amorous feelings at Śiva's person. Thereupon, Śiva became furious and hurled his trident at Kāmadeva and killed him. Since then the trident has remained erect at Gopeshwar.

# 3

## *ART OF GOPESHWAR*

We have seen that Gopeshwar was already an important religious centre in sixth-seventh century AD. Gaṇapatināga set up an iron trident here in honour of Śiva. However, extant temples at Gopeshwar date from the eighth century AD. It is likely that the main temple was constructed at the same site where the original temple of Śiva was built, in honor of which Gaṇapatināga set up the trident under reference. In some Nāgarī inscriptions, referred to above, the site is mentioned as "Gopasthala" (place of cowherds). It is likely that the site remained under the supervision of cowherds at some point in time. Alternatively, originally the Gopeshwar area may have been settled by the cowherds hence called Gopasthala. In this connection it is to be noted that even today its forested surroundings are rich in pastureland called "*kharka*". Interestingly, according to a local tradition when King Sagara was ruling in this region, one of his cow used to drop her milk at the spot where the present *svayambhu linga* (natural rock) is consecrated, and therefore could not yield any milk for the king. It is said that when the king learned that the milch cow under reference was not yielding milk he chased the activities of the cow, and found that the cow dropped her milk at a particular spot on a *svayambhu liṅga*. That is how the king learned about the presence of the holy site of Gopeshwar and erected a temple there. Thus this tradition also suggests association of Gopeshwar with cow.

Gopeshwar appears to have been a major temple site. The presence of some twenty-one *āmalasārakas* of different sizes found within the compound of the main temple site, obviously originally each crowned the *Śikhara* of a Nāgara temple, bespeaks the architectural richness of this site. The main temple, known as Gopeshwar is dedicated to Śiva, the object of worship being a *svayambhu-linga* (Pl.14). It is built in Nāgara style with a *latin Śikhara*. *Triratha* on plan, the *Śikhara* of the temple is adorned with *chaitya* motif all over, hence termed as *jāla Śikhara* in architectural canons (Pls. 15,16 & 17). Some of these *chaitya* motifs are adorned with *bhadramukhas*. The *chandrasala* of its tall *Śukanāsa* shows Śiva in his Naṭarāja aspect. Stylistically, this temple has close similarity with the Mrityunjaya temple, Jageshwar (Almora), both in terms of plan and elevation as well as ornamentation. Palaeographically, Mrityunjaya temple has been dated to eighth century AD, therefore the temple at Gopeshwar can also be assigned to the same date. The *gūḍdhamaṇḍapa* of the main temple is a later addition. Besides, there are three smaller shrines, one of which is of *valabhi* style, stylistically assignable to tenth century AD. Architecturally, these temples are similar to the Katyūrī temples found all over Uttarakhand. The sculptures of Gopeshwar represent the true regional art style of Uttarakhand called the Katyūrī art (Joshi 1989a). In the following section of this monograph the representative types of sculptures that show different phases of the Katyūrī art have been illustrated.

Introducing the art of Uttarakhand Joshi (1989a) has outlined the following salient features of the Katyūrī art:

1. Preceding this art activity, no important art tradition is evidenced in this region, as a result of which in its earlier stages the Katyūrī art drew inspiration from the classical Gupta art.

2. With a few exceptions showing kings, that too in metal, all the sculptures belonging to this art depict different Brahmanical deities with simple iconographic forms, complicated or enigmatic forms being almost absent. Significantly, Jain and Buddhist images are rare and belong to a later period. In our opinion their attribution to Katyūrī art is doubtful.

3. Sculptures belonging to Katyūrī art are found in thousands within the territorial limits of the Katyūrī kingdom comprising the whole of UP hills and adjoining western Nepal, and date between C. 650-1200 A.D.

4. These sculptures are made of locally available stone of different varieties, as a result of which there is a marked difference in the treatment of surface. Depending upon the nature of stone, in a few examples it is very smooth and lustrous and in others it is rough and coarse.

5. These sculptures are executed frontally in relief. Only metal sculptures are treated in round.

6. Only a solitary example of wooden sculpture belonging to the Katyūrī art has survived. Since wooden architecture has prevailed in later times in the region under study, the

same may hold good during the Katyūrī times. The wooden architecture of the adjoining Himachal Pradesh is a pointer in this regard.

7. Some amount of ethnic elements may also be noticed in this art, for example, full sleeve jacket-like garment worn by the female figures, a special type of apron-like dress worn by Sūrya and his attendants, etc., which are still in vogue in the interior of this region. It is interesting to note in this connection that Sūrya is a very popular deity in Katyūrī art, obviously in the cold climate of hills, warming sun-rays are most welcome. Whereas Indra, the god of rain, is seldom represented, for we have frequent local rains in the Himalayas which produce chill even during the summer. Under these circumstances Sūrya was preferred to Indra. Interestingly, the Sāyana-mūrtis of Vishṇu are frequently placed alongside water springs with the belief that Vishnu has his abode in waters, and that so long as Vishnu image remains situated alongside the water springs there will be water in it. Besides, the presence of Vishṇu image added to the sanctity of the reservoir. It not only served as a check to wanton use of water, but also obliged people to keep it clean.

8. Human form in Katyūrī art is attractive and graceful with a slim body and a somewhat U-sḥaped plump face wrought with contemplative serenity. Devoid of showy dress and ornaments, the sculptures in Katyūrī art display a touch of naturalism and create an aura of spiritual illumination and sublimity.

It is worthwhile to add here that art activities in stone in Central Himalayas have a hoary antiquity. Thus, some of the schematic representations of triangles, dots, circles, foot-prints, outline of a cat-like animal engraved on the rocks associated with certain early burial sites may date back to the prehistoric times (Carnac 1877; Joshi 1987; 1988; 1995; Mathpal 1987; 1992). The earliest art objects in stone belonging to the historical period found in Central Himalayas are the standing *Yaksha* and *Yakshi* figures at Bharat Mandir, Rishikesh (Katoch 1982: 79, Pl. 12.36), and railing pillars showing "beautiful *mithuna* figures *Yaksha*, *Yakshi* and *Kichaka gana* in relief with traces of upper and lower miniature rail borders" (*IAR 1971-72*: 80), datable between circa second century BC and first century AD, followed by *sthānaka* Vishnu and Harihara images from Triyugi Narayan (Chamoli) dated to third century AD (Tiwari 1983: Pls. 41-42) and *sthānaka* Vishnu from Nakulesvar (District Pithoragarh) dated to fourth century AD (Joshi 1980). These sculptures seem to have been imported, most probably from Mathura, for they are made from such a variety of sandstone as is not found locally.

The earliest example of locally executed stone sculpture is the almost life-size image of a *Yaksha* seated in *paryaṅkāsana* (European fashion) on a stool found at Jaskot (Almora). It compares well with the Mathura sculptures of Kushāṇa kings seated on throne. On stylistic grounds it has been dated to circa third century AD (Joshi 1981). Next in order of chronology are three sculptures from Lakhamandal (Vats and Agrawal 1944) and one from Kashipur (Nautiyal 1969: 154-56). The Lakhamandal sculptures depict standing figures of Jaya and Vijaya, and Umā-sahita Vīṇadhara-mūrti of Śiva. The Kashipur figure depicts Trivikrama Vishnu. Stylistically, these sculptures belong to the late Gupta art, and have been dated to sixth century AD. It may be noted here that these sculptures are found in

Dun and Terai-Bhabhar region of Central Himalayas which are relatively closer to Mathura art. Significantly, in the interior hills of Central Himalayas, Gopeshwar is the only site where we find five sculptures belonging to the late Gupta art executed in local stone, namely, the river goddesses Ganga (Pl. 18), Yamuna (Pl. 19), two-armed Śaivite male figure (Pl. 20), *Yakshī* (Pl. 21), and *mithuna* figures (Pl. 22). The presence of these sculptures in Central Himalayas clearly proves that these art objects have been inspired by the Gupta art, hence significant. In this connection Joshi rightly observes that the Katyūrīs, being resourceful, invited master artists from the plains of India in the initial stage and, in course of time, these artists developed an art idiom of their own under the Katyūrīs patronage.

Stylistically, the above-mentioned art objects found in Uttarakhand bear close resemblance with some of the late Gupta sculptures in general and the ones found at Ahichchhatra and Dewalgarh in particular. Obviously, the regional art idiom of Uttarakhand that developed in the following centuries was inspired by the Gupta art as is evident from the extant examples. In this connection Joshi (1989b: 17-28) adds "It is for this reason that we find a family likeness in the early Katyūrī art and the contemporary early medieval art of Northern India. The characteristic features of this phase are restraint in ornamentation, tasteful but simple treatment of hair-style, ornamentation and drapery. The plasticity in this stage may be seen in the flowing contours of body with rounded form tending to fuse in the background of the relief. The figures are youthful and serene and often give a feeling of lightness, softness and subtleness. Representation of diminutive figures accompanying the main deity/deities is fewest. The sculptures belonging to this phase depict Brahmanical deities, invariably in stone in relief, and may be placed between the latter half of the seventh and eighth century A.D."

The early sculptures from Gopeshwar remarkably conform to Joshi's above characterization of the beginning of the Katyūrī art, as may be seen in the reliefs depicting Harihara (Pl. 23), male figure holding a fluted bowl (Pl. 24), the mother goddesses (Pls. 25-31), Vīrarbhadra Śiva (Pl. 32), Gaja-lakshmī (Pl. 33), Vinādhara Śiva (Pl. 34), and the four-armed female deity (Pl. 35). These sculptures bear close similarity with the ones described earlier, but for the elegant treatment of dress and ornaments, considerable plasticity and natural roundness of bodily contour. Nevertheless, these early sculptures dated to seventh and early eighth centuries mark the beginning of the Katyūrī art, which develops into an art idiom of its own subsequently in the second phase, examples of which are found in large numbers all over Uttarakhand (Nautiyal 1969; Joshi 1970; 1989b; Tiwari 1983; Kathoch 1981; 1996; 200; Khanduri 1994). According to Joshi, this phase of the Katyūrī art "shows florescence", the characteristic features of which are as follows:

- Intricately sculptured human form and somewhat stereotyped execution of hair-style, drapery and ornaments.
- The contours tend to be linear and angular, sometimes causing stiffness in human form which is further increased by comparatively extravagant jewellery.
- A noteworthy feature of this phase is the touch of naturalism resulting in the production of several lively sculptures. This is also true of the first phase as well.

- Furthermore, sculptures with narrative or iconographic orientation are pregnant with expression and are distinctly harmonious. The artist has taken great care to create an aura of spiritual illumination and sublimity in the overall execution of these sculptures. Apart from divine figures, kings or royal persons are also depicted in this phase.

These characteristic features of the sècond phase of the Katyūrī art are clearly noticeable in Gopeshwar sculptures datable between later half of the eighth and tenth centuries AD. Thus, some examples though carrying traits of earlier phase, such as simple treatment of ornamentation, roundness and naturalism, show somewhat stylization in hairstyle and drapery, and stiffness in human form, for example, Śurya (Pl. 36), Nandi (Pl. 37), Umā-Maheśvara (Pl. 38), Lakulīśa (Pl. 39), Kārttikeya (Pls. 40-42), and Śiva (Pl.43); the intricate chisel work and somewhat linear and angular bodily contour may be seen in the sculptures representing Indra (Pl. 44), Śiva (Pl. 45), Śurya (Pls. 46-47), Pārvatī (Pl. 48), Vishṇu (Pl. 49), *Chaturmukha linga* (Pl. 50), Vishṇu (Pl. 51-53), Umā-Maheśvara (Pl. 54). In this phase, one badly restore metal image of Vishnu is found, the extend original part of which bear family likeness with the *sthanaka* bronze image of Vishnu reported earlier (Pl. 55). Interestingly, in executing these images the sculptors have been successful in creating "an aura of spiritual illumination and sublimity".

The third and the last phase of the Katyūrī art is represented by sculptures belonging to eleventh century AD onwards. According to Joshi (1989b):

Third stage that marks decadence is noticed in the sculptures datable to eleventh and twelfth centuries. There are distinctly two varieties of sculptures in this stage.

The first variety displays intricate chisel work in the treatment of drapery and ornamentation. There is a tendency to crowd the relief with attendant diminutive figures. It seems that in producing these sculptures the sculptor was more interested in the details of dress and ornaments than the actual figures, so much so that in many examples the ornaments become superfluous. These sculptures are highly stylized and lack in harmony in most of the examples. Human body is depicted without any bend which further adds to the stiffness and heaviness of the form.

In the second variety of the third stage the sculpture is not crowded with attendant figures. There is restraint in ornamentation. However, the sculptures lack in vitality and harmony. Treatment of figures -whether anthropomorphic or theomorphic in this variety is rough and devoid of roundness. Instead, it develops into a somewhat flat composition which adds to the stiffness of an already stylized figure.

Joshi's suggestions are remarkably supported by the Gopeshwar evidence. Thus, the first variety of Joshi's third stage is represented by Pārvatī (Pl. 56), Umā-Maheśvara (Pls. 57-58), and Śūrya (Pl. 59). These sculptures display intricate chisel work resulting in stiffness and heaviness of bodily form. The second variety may be identified in sculptures showing Nataraja Śiva (Pl. 60) and Durgā (Pl. 61). These sculptures show restraint in ornamentation, but it is somewhat flattish in composition and highly stylized, hence lack in plasticity and naturalism.

There are also a few examples of post- Katyūrī art in Gopeshwar, which appear "a continuum of the degenerate Katyūrī art". They are extremely stylized, the bodily form is flattish, bulky and stiff, for example, Nandī (Pl. 62), and standing male figures (Pls. 63-64), some of these lack in third dimensional effect on account of extremely flattened surface as is evident from part of a door-frame (Pl. 65).

# 4

# *ICONOGRAPHIC DETAILS OF SCULPTURES*

## RIVER GODDESS GAṄGĀ (Pl. 18)
**Late Sixth Century AD**

Two-armed figure of the river goddess Gaṅgā standing on her mount *makara*. On her right is shown a diminutive attendant carrying a *chhatra* (parasol). However, the sculpture is irreparably damaged. Nevertheless, the horizontally pleated folds of the *sari*, long necklace and elegant *tribhaṇga* standing pose of the goddess display high quality of plastic art of the Gupta Age.

## RIVER GODDESS YAMUNĀ (Pl. 19)
**Sixth Century AD**

The sculpture showing two-armed figure of the river goddess Yamunā standing in *tribhaṇga* pose is stylistically akin to the one described above. She wears ear ornaments, short beaded and long chain like necklaces, anklets, a tight bejewelled waist-band supports her long *sari*, while a girdle hangs loosely forming a loop. To her left is a diminutive figure of an umbrella bearer. The sculpture is badly vandalized.

## ŚAIVITE DEITY (Pl. 20)
**Sixth Century AD**

Two-armed male figure standing in *abhaṇga* pose. His matted hair is arranged in loops. He wears ear ornaments, *hansulī*, *sarpa-mālā*, ornate armlets, wristlets, a loose waist band, and a *dhoti* secured with a beaded girdle. The left hand of the figure is akimbo, while the corresponding right one holds a long weapon, only shaft of which is intact. This beautiful sculpture stands badly mutilated. Stylistically, the sculpture bears close affinity to the Gupta art.

## YAKSHĪ (Pl. 21)
**Sixth Century A.D.**

Standing image of a female figure (*yakshī?*) forming an architectural member. Her hair is done in a top chignon. She is adorned with ear-ornament, a torque, wristlets, and a *sari* secured at the waist by a *mekhalā*. Her right hand rests on a creeper which passes through her arm above her shoulder. In her upraised right hand she holds a conical object (fire?). There is plasticity in the execution of this relief.

## MITHUNA FIGURES (Pl. 22)
**Sixth Century AD**

Architectural member depicting in low relief *mithuna* figures standing under a tree within a niche which is surmounted by a mesh of *chaitya*-arches and geometrical motives. The male figure on the left is shown as caressing the female figure's breast with his right hand while his left hand is placed on her back. The female figure embraces the male figure with her right hand while her left hand is akimbo. She stands in a reposeful posture with her bent left leg resting on the ground on her toe. Crouching figure below in the act of supporting the niche on his upraised hands flanked by two lion-faced seated figures shown frontally are also depicted.

**HARIHARA (Pl. 23)**
**Sixth Century AD**

The syncretic image of four-armed Harihara represents Hara (Śiva) in the proper right half and Hari (Vishṇu) in the left one. Hara aspect is suggested by the matted hairdo (*jaṭājūṭa*) studded with a crescent, and Hari by the *kirīṭa* crown. The figure is adorned with ear-ornaments, an *ekāvalī*, wristlets, and a *dhoti* secured at the waist by a bejewelled girdle. The sculpture is badly mutilated.

**MALE DEVOTEE (Pl. 24)**
**Sixth Century AD**

The sculpture shows two-armed male figure broken below the bust. He holds a bowl-shaped fluted lamp (?) with both hands raised up to the level of his waist. The figure is adorned with short and long necklaces, armlets and ear ornaments. His matted hair is tastefully done in a top chignon tied with a fillet.

**INDRĀṆI (Pl. 25)**
**Seventh Century A.D.**

The sculpture shows two-armed image of Indrāṇī seated in *paryaṇkasana* (European fashion) on the back of a crouching elephant. She wears long *kuṇḍalas* (ear-rings), a torque and wristlets. Her hair is done in a top chignon. Her breasts are covered with a *stanottarīya*, and she wears a *sari*. Her right hand holds an indistinct stick-like object (a local conception of *vajra*?) entwined with a rosary, and the left one holds a baby seated on her lap, suggestive of her *mātrikā* aspect.

**CHĀMUṆĪA (Pl. 26)**
**Seventh Century A.D**

The sculpture shows four-armed Chāmuṇḍa seated in *paryaṅkāsana* (European fashion). Her emaciated body with protruding tongue gives a ferocious look as enjoined in the iconographic texts (cf. Banerjea 1956: 505, 507-08). Her hair, arranged in top chignon, is adorned with human skulls. She wears long *kuṇḍalas* (ear-rings). She holds an indistinct object in her upper right hand and a bell in the upper left one, while with her lower hands she is shown seizing the foot and hair of a two-armed human figure. The human figure holds a dagger in his right hand as if fighting the goddess. According to the *Mārkaṇḍeya purāṇa* (83. 1-7) the emaciated goddess sprang from the forehead of goddess Ambikā to kill demons Chaṇḍa and Muṇḍa. Hence she was named Chāmuṇḍa (*ibid* 83.8-24). It seems that in this sculpture Chāmuṇḍa is shown as vanquishing one of the aforementioned demons.

**VĀRĀHĪ (Pl. 27)**
**Seventh Century A.D.**

The relief depicts four-armed sow-faced Vārāhī seated in *paryaṅkāsana* (European fashion) on the back of a buffalo. Clockwise, from lower right hand to lower left one, she holds a bell, a fish, and an indistinct object (a pie of flesh?) attached to sow's snout, as if being eaten and a baby respectively. It is also to be noted that a creeper surmounted by a flower is also shown issuing from her upper right hand. The goddess wears ear-rings, a torque and a long necklace. Her hair is arranged in a top chignon. It is interesting to note that here the attributes of the upper hands of the goddess seem to carry tantric influence, for *matsya* (fish) and *māṁsa* (flesh) are two of the five *pañcha-makāra* tantric traits, the rest three being *mudrā*, *madirā* and *maithuna* (Banerjea 1956: 506).

## VAISHṆAVĪ (Pl. 28)
**Seventh Century A.D.**

The four-armed image of Vaishṇavī reproduced here shows the goddess seated in *paryaṅkāsana* on Garuda with spread wings. She is adorned with long *kuṇḍalas* (ear-rings), a torque, wristlets, *stanottarīya* and *sari*. The deity holds a *chakra* and a stylized flower (*padma?*) respectively in her upper right and left hands, and a *śaṁkha* in the lower right one, while the corresponding left hand is shown as holding the head of a reclining baby.

## KAUMĀRĪ (Pl. 29)
**Seventh Century A.D.**

The two-armed image of Kaumārī illustrated here shows her seated in *paryaṅkāsana* (European fashion). Her hair is arranged in top chignon. She wears a *huḍuka* (hourglass shaped drum) like curious ear ornaments, a torque, anklets, a *stanottarīya*, a waist band and *sari*. She seems to feed her mount peacock with her right hand, while her left hand holds an indistinct object.

## BRAHMĀṆĪ (Pl. 30)
## Seventh Century A.D.

The two-armed image of Brahmāṇī reproduced here shows her seated on a lotus-seat in *paryaṅkāsana* (European fashion). It is likely that the lotus-seat in fact represents a stylized pair of geese, as is noticed in the sculptural art of Uttarakhand. The deity is adorned with long ear ornaments, torque and wristlets. She also wears *stanottarīya* and *sari*. Her upraised right hand shows *akshamālā*-cum *abhaya* pose, while in her left hand, resting on her knee, she holds a *pothi* above which an indistinct object is also shown (pomegranate?).

## MAHEŚVARĪ (Pl. 31)
## Seventh Century AD

The relief shows two-armed image of Mahesvarī seated on Nandi in *paryaṅkāsana* (European fashion). She is wearing long ear ornaments, a torque, wristlets, anklets, *stanottarīya* and *sari*. She holds a trident in her right hand and a *śriphala*(?) in the left one.

## VĪRABHADRA-ŚIVA (Pl.32)
## Seventh Century AD

The relief shows standing four-armed and three-eyed ithyphallic figure of Śiva. His matted hair is arranged in top chignon. He wears a *huḍuka* (hourglass-shaped drum) like curious ear ornament in his right ear and a simple long ear-ring in the left one. In addition, he is adorned with wristlets, a short *yajñopavīta* and a short *dhoti*. Interestingly, his penis erectus in also shown prominently. His front hand holds a *viṇā* and the back right and left ones a bell and a serpent with raised hood respectively. Since iconographic texts enjoin that *Sapta mātrikās* should be accompanied with Vīrabhadra and Gaṇeśa (Banerjea 1956 : 505), it is reasonable to identify the standing image of Śiva with Vīrabhadra. According to Banerji (1956: 505) in the iconographic texts, the above described goddesses form the stereotyped list of the *sapta matṛikās*. The image of Gaṇeśa, however, was not found among these eight sculptures.

**GAJALAKSHMĪ (Pl. 33)**
**Eighth Century AD**

The broken relief shows two armed Lakshmī being anointed by two flanking elephants each standing on a lotus issuing from a creeper studded with lotus buds. The goddess wears a top chignon adorned with a beaded hair-band, ear ornaments, *ekāvalī*, wristlets, an elaborate girdle supporting the lower-garment and *stanottarīya* covering her breast. Her right hand is broken. In her raised left hand she holds a creeper surmounted by a full bloom lotus. The sculpture is remarkable for its plasticity and contemplative expression of Lakshmi's face.

**SIVA NAṬARĀJA (Pl. 34)**
**Eighth Century AD**

The relief depicts four-armed image of Śiva as Naṭarāja. He wears *jaṭā-mukuṭa*, ear ornaments, a torque, *graiveyaka*, armlets, wristlets, girdle and a short *dhoti*. He holds a *khaṭ vāṅga* in his upper right hand, a snake in the corresponding left one while his front hands hold vīṇā. A diminutive *ghaṭa player* is seated on the right side of Naṭarāja, and a similar figure playing on cymbals (?) to his left.

## PĀRVATĪ (Pl. 35)
## Eighth Century AD

Four-armed female deity (Pārvatī?) seated in *Utkuṭikāsana*. Her hair is tastefully arranged in tresses, some falling on her shoulders others done in top chignon. She wears multi-stringed dear-skin like upper garment and a *sari* as the lower garment. She holds a lotus stalk in either upraised hands, while her lower hands, resting on the knees, are broken. It seems that the image represents the *tapaśvinī* aspect of Pārvatī.

## SŪRYA (Pl. 36)
## Eighth Century AD

The relief shows two-armed image of Sūrya standing in *samabhaṅga* pose and holding a stalk of full bloom lotus in either hand. His hair is done in six tresses, three on either sides, falling over his shoulders. He wears a high *karanda*, ear ornaments, wristlets, a short necklace (*ekāvali*), a girdle, an *avyaṅga* with a sword tucked on proper left, *luṅgī*-like(?) lower garment, high boots and a *dupaṭṭā*. He is flanked by his two attendants one of which on his right side is Piṅgala. The other side of the relief is broken.

## NANDĪ (Pl. 37)
## Eighth Century AD

The sculpture, fully in round, shows crouchant Nandī with a garland of bells passing round his prominent hump. Multiple lines in relief looking like a collar are suggestive of a dewlap.

## UMĀ-SAHITA VĪNADHARAMŪRTI (Pl. 38)
**Late Eighth Early Ninth Century AD**

Fixed on the back gate of the temple the relief depicts Śiva seated in *lalitāsana*. The four-armed god holds a *vīnā* in his front hands and a serpent in his back right, his back left hand, embracing Pārvatī, rests on her left shoulder. Two-armed Pārvatī holds a mirror in her left hand, while her right hand, passing from behind Śiva's back, is kept on the right shoulder of the god in the act of embracing. Below the divine couple are shown diminutive figures of seated *Gaṇeśa* in the left, crouching Nandī looking at the divine couple in the middle, and Karttikeya in the right. The divine couple wears matted hair, stylish earrings, neck ornaments, armlets, wristlets and lower garments secured with girdles.

## LAKULĪŚA (Pl. 39)
**Late Eighth Early Ninth Century AD**

Four-armed ithyphallic Lakulīśa seated in *padmāsana* on a high pedestal. His matted hair is done in a fan-shaped chignon. He holds a *bījāpūraka* fruit in his back right hand resting on his right knee, the corresponding left hand holds a *lakuṭa*. His front hands are raised up in *vyākhyāna mudrā*. Below him are four (?) seated human figures most probably representing his four disciples, namely Kuśika, Mitra, Garga and Kaurushya. The sculpture is badly mutilated.

## KĀRTIKEYA (Pl. 40)
**Late Eighth Early Ninth Century AD**

Two-armed image of Kārtikeya holding a spear in his upraised right hand. His left hand is akimbo. The god's mount peacock is shown on his left with his feathers spread behind the deity in the lower half of the relief. The youthful figure of god is shown with his typical hairdo divided into three parts secured by a hairband. He is adorned with ear, neck, arm and wrist ornaments, a short dhoti, a loose girdle, and a loose loin cloth forming a loop in front.

**KĀRTIKEYA (Pl. 41)**
**Late Eighth Early Ninth Century AD**

The mutilated relief shows a two-armed male figure (Kārtikeya) standing in *tribhaṇga* posture. He holds a spear(?) in his right hand, the left one is akimbo(?). The figure is shown with an interesting neck ornament consisting of three pendants, stylish lion cloth, and a girdle.

**KĀRTIKEYA (Pl. 42)**
**Late Eighth Early Ninth Century AD**

Two-armed Kārtikeya seated on his mount peacock. He holds a spear in his raised right hand, and his left hand feeds his mount peacock. His hair, done in *trisikhā* (three-tresses) is secured by a bejewelled hair band. The god wears ear-rings, short necklace, armlets, wristlets and a *dhoti*. The background of relief is stylistically ornamented with the feathers of peacock spread all over in different directions.

**ŚIVA (Pl. 43)**
**Late Eighth Early Ninth Century AD**

Two-armed standing male deity (Śiva?) holding a *paraśu* in his left hand, and the right one is raised up in *abhaya* pose. He is adorned with *jaṭā-mukuṭa*, ear ornaments and an *ekāvalī*. His *dhoti* is secured at the waist by an elaborate girdle. The sculpture is badly obliterated.

**INDRA (under worship) (Pl. 44)**
**Late Eighth Early Ninth Century AD**

Two-armed image of Indra seated on his mount elephant in *mahārāja-līlāsana*. Both of his mutilated hands rest on his knees. He is flanked by four diminutive female figures, two on either side. These may be identified with *apsarās* whose lord is Indra. The god wears elaborate dress and ornaments appropriate to his person as king of Gods. His hair is tastefully arranged in curly tresses in the background of which is shown a highly ornate halo. The sculpture is a representative example of Katyūrī art.

**ŚIVA (Pl. 45)**
**Late Eighth Early Ninth Century AD**

Two-armed and three-eyed male figure of Śiva standing in *samapāda* posture. His matted hair is arranged aesthetically in a top chignon secured with a bejewelled hair-band. He wears an *ekāvalī*, ear ornaments, armlets and wristlets. His short *dhoti* is secured with a girdle. His right hand raised up to the level of his breast holds a *paraśu*(?); the corresponding left one, somewhat akimbo, rests on the knot of his loosely worn waist-band close to the left thigh of the standing figure. The image is further enriched with an ornate halo showing intricate scroll motif.

**SŪRYA (Pl. 46)**
**Late Eighth Early Ninth Century AD**

Two-armed image of sūrya standing in *samabhaṅga* pose and holding a stalk of full bloom lotus in ether upraised hand. Sun is adorned with a *karanda*-type cap, ear ornaments, a torque, a *yajñopovīta*, wristlets, and an ornamented girdle with a sword/ dagger tucked on proper right side and an *avyanga* (woollen thread). He wears a *luṅgī*-like lower garment and high boots. Flanking him on his right is Piṅgala and Daṇḍī on his left, both wearing identical dress and ornaments in the same style as the main deity.

**SŪRYA (Pl. 47)**
**Late Eighth Early Ninth Century AD**

Two-armed sūrya holding a bunch of lotus flowers in each hand raised up to the waist level. Flanked by Piṅgala on his right and Daṅḍī on his left, the god stands on the background of an ornate lotus-shaped halo. He is shown as wearing a *karanda*-like head-dress. His hair is arranged in tresses falling over his shoulders. The god is adorned with ear, neck and wrist ornaments, an ornamented girdle and an *avyaṅga*. In addition, he wears a *luṅgī*-like lower garment and high boots. His attendants are dressed in a somewhat similar style as the main deity himself.

**PĀRVATĪ (Pl. 48)**
**Late Ninth Century AD**

Four-armed standing image of Pārvatī showing an *akshamālā* in her upper right hand, a serpent in the corresponding left one, a *kamaṇḍala* in the lower left hand, while the lower right one is broken. The entire relief is badly mutilated.

**VISHṆU (Pl.49)**
**Ninth Century A.D.**

The four-armed bronze reproduced here was first described by M.C. Joshi (1970). However, its present whereabouts are not known. He assigns it to ninth century. The sculpture shows four-armed Sthānaka Vishṇu with a simple radiating śirashchakra. He is decked with an elaborate *kirīṭa*, *karṇa-phūla*, *ekavalī*, *vanamālā*, *yajñopavīta*, armlets, girdle and anklets. His front right hand holds a *padma*, and the corresponding left one a saṁkha; while the back right rests on the heads of personified figure of Gadā-devī, and the back left one on the head of Chakra-purusha. The flanking personified āyudha-purushas are decked like the central deity. The sculpture bears a family likeness with the famous Pona image from Jageshwar (Joshi 1976).

**CHATURMUKH SIVA LING (Pl. 50)**
**Late Ninth Century AD**

Chaturmukha *linga* showing Aghora aspect of Śiva in the *Rudra-bhāga*. The god's matted hair is arranged in a chignon secured by a beaded string with a medallion. The matted hair carrying the crescent is encircled by a serpent. The fierce aspect of god is represented by canine and prominent moustache.

**VISHṆU (Pl. 51)**
**Late Ninth Century AD**

Four-armed *sthānaka* Vishṇu image shown in *samapāda* pose. Vishnu's hair is arranged in tresses which fall over his shoulders. He wears a *kirīta*, ear and neck ornaments, wristlets, a *yajñapavita*, a *vanamālā* and a *dhoti* secured with a girdle. The god holds a full bloom lotus and a conch in his respective front right and left hands. His back right hand is broken while the remaining left seems to rest on the head of an attendant figure, most probably one of his āyudha-purushas.

**VISHṆU (Pl. 52)**
**Late Ninth Century AD**

The relief shows four-armed *sthānaka* Vishṇu, wearing a *kirīta*, ear-ornaments, a torque, a *vanamālā* and a *dhoti* secured with a girdle. In his upper right hand he holds a mace, in the corresponding left one a *chakra*, the lower right one raised upto the shoulder is broken, while the lower left one, holding a *śamkha*, is akimbo. The relief is broken below the knees.

**VISHṆU (Pl. 53)**
**Tenth Century AD**

Four-armed *sthānaka* Vishnu image standing in *samapada* pose. The god wears an ornate *kirīṭa* with his hair arranged in tresses falling over his shoulders. He is adorned with ear and neck ornaments, wristlẹts, *yajñopovīta*, a *vanamālā* and a short *dhoti* secured with a girdle. His front right hand holds a full bloom lotus, the corresponding left a conch, his back right hand rests on the head of *Gadā-devī* (personified mace) and the remaining one on the head of *Chakra purusha* (personified wheel).

## UMĀ-MAHEŚVARA (Pl. 54)
**Tenth Century AD**

Four-armed Śiva seated in *lalitāsana*. He holds a snake in his upper right hand while his lower right hand rests on the hand of a diminutive female (?) figure. His upper left hand holds a flower, and with his lower left he caresses Pārvatī's chin, who sits on his left leg. Two-armed Pārvatī holds a mirror (?) in her left hand, while her right hand rests on the left foot of Śiva. The divine couple is adorned with dress and ornaments appropriate to their persons. There are three diminutive figures below the seat of Umā-Maheśvara: Gaṇeśa seated in *śukhāsana* in the left, crouching Nandī in the middle, and Kārttikeya on his mount peacock in the right.

## METAL IMAGE (Pl. 55)
**Tenth-Eleventh Century**

Metal image depicts a human figure standing on a low seat. The sculpture is badly damaged and has been subjected to awkward restoration as evidenced in the assembly of original head and lower portion of the body below the waist on a crudely cast torso and attached hands. The extant original parts of this sculpture bear family likeness with the *sthānaka* bronze image of Vishnu earlier reported from Gopeshwar (Nautiyal 1969: Joshi, M.C.1970) in respect of ornamentation, particularly the elaborate girdle supporting the short *dhoti*. However, the facial expression and the *śiraśhchakra* (nimbus) are indicative of stylization. Nevertheless the metallurgical skill of the sculpture is praiseworthy as evidenced in slightly bent lower portion showing naturalism.

**PĀRVATĪ (Pl. 56)**
**Eleventh Century AD**

Four-armed image of Pārvatī standing in *sambhaṅga* pose. Devī wears an elaborate *jaṭāmukuṭa*, earrings, long necklace with a floral pendant, *stanottarīya* (covering her breasts), and a highly ornate *sari*. Her upper right hand is holding agni-cum-*akshmālā*, while the lower one is in *varadā mudra*, the upper left is broken and the lower left hand holds a water pot (*kamaṇḍalu*). She is flanked by two female attendants (*chaurī*-bearer) standing in *tribhanga* posture. Diminutive figures of a lion and a deer sitting below on her right and left sides respectively are also shown. Interestingly a *godha* (iguana) is also depicted on the pedestal of the relief. The relief depicts the *tapasvinī* aspect of Pārvatī.

**UMĀ-MAHEŚVARA (Pl. 57)**
**Eleventh Century AD**

Four-armed Śiva seated in *lalitāsana*. His matted hair is arranged in loops supported by a bejewelled hairband. He wears ear and neck ornaments and a short *dhoti* secured with a girdle. All of his hands are broken. To his left is shown his consort Umā seated on the left leg of Śiva. Below the divine couple crouching Nandi and two diminutive figures are also shown. The relief is badly damaged.

**UMĀ-MAHEŚVARA (Pl. 58)**
**10th -11th Century AD**

The relief depicts Umā-Maheśvara in stylized pose. Four-armed Śiva is seated in *lalitāsana*. He holds a trident in his back right hand and a flower in the front right one. Both of his left hands pass behind Pārvatī's back, the upper left holding a serpent, while the other one rests on the left shoulder of Pārvatī. Two-armed Pārvatī, seated on the left leg of Śiva, holds a mirror(?) in her left hand and her right hand, passing behind Śiva's back, is kept on the waist of the god in the act of embracing him. The divine couple is dressed with ornaments appropriate to their persons; in addition Pārvatī wears a *dupaṭṭā* with its fluttering left end falling from the left arm of the goddess.

## SŪRYA (Pl. 59)
**Twelfth Century AD**

Two-armed image of Sūrya standing in *samabhaṅga* pose and holding a full bloom lotus in each of the upraised hands. The god is adorned with *karanda*, ear, arm and neck ornaments, a girdle and an *avyaṅga*. He wears a *dhoti*, high pointed boots and a coat of mail. The god is flanked by four human figures, two on either side. Figures shown in the foreground represent Daṇḍī on proper left and Piṅgala on proper right of the god. Behind these male figures are two female figures each holding a sun flower(?) in one of the hands, while the other hand is akimbo, probably representing his consorts Rājñī and Nishprabhā. The relief also depicts two garland bearing *vidyādharas* above.

## VINĀDHARA NATARAJA (Pl. 60)
**Thirteenth Century AD**

Ten-armed Viṇādhara Naṭarāja holding a *vīṇa* in his front hands. His lowest right hand is broken, in the remaining ones, clockwise from the lower right, he holds a trident, a serpent, a *ḍamaru* a shield, a *khaṭvāṅga*, a bow and a bowl. A diminutive figure playing on drum is seated on the right of Śiva, another one playing on cymbals stands to his left. Immediately in front of the latter is shown Nandī with his head turned towards Naṭ arāja. Śiva is adorned with head, ear, and neck ornaments, armlets, wristlets, girdle and a long garland. The upper right and left corner of the relief are occupied by garland bearing *vidyādharas*.

### DURGĀ (Pl. 61)
### Thirteenth Century A.D.

Six-armed image of Durgā seated on lion in *utkuṭikāsana*. She is adorned with an elaborate *jaṭāmukuṭa*. She wears *kuṇḍalas* and neck ornaments, *yajñopavīta*, wristlets, a loose girdle, and a *sari* as a lower garment. She holds clockwise from the lowest right hand, a *chakra*, a sword, a disk, a bell and a bow.

### NANDI (Pl. 62)
### Fourteenth Century AD

Crouching Nandī with a garland of bells passing round his hump, in addition to a neck ornament and a saddle with ornamental border. The sculpture is in round.

### STANDING MALE FIGURE (Pl. 63)
### Fourteenth Century AD

Two-armed standing male figure holding(?) some indistinct object (a bowl shaped lamp?) on his hands raised to the level of the waist. He sports a bun-shaped hairdo, ear and neck ornaments, a *dhoti* and a long *dupaṭṭā* whose both ends are falling a little above the ankles. The figure is badly mutilated.

## STANDING MALE FIGURE (Pl. 64)
**Fourteenth Century AD**

Two-armed standing male figure with left hand trampling a diminutive figure. His right hand is broken and in his left hand, raised above, holds a flower(?). He wears a long *vanamālā* and ear-ornaments. The relief bears a heavy coat of vermillion, which being the periodical votive offering by devotees who identify it as Hanumāna. If the identification is correct the diminutive figure represents a demon.

## DVĀRAŚĀKHĀ (Pl. 65)
**Fourteenth Century AD**

Architectural member forming a part of a door frame represents a *dvāraśākhā* depicting three figures in a vertical row. At the top, a male figure is standing on a raised seat, his right hand holds a flower bud(?) and the left one a staff with a *patākā*, in the middle, a male figure standing erect, wearing a conical head-dress and holding an arrow in the right hand and a bow in the left one. Below, a female figure (river goddess?) standing in *abhaṇga* posture. She holds a water pot in her upraised left hand and a *chaurī* (fly whisk) in the left one. She wears a basket type headgear, thick necklace, *ekāvalī*, earrings and lower garments. The goddess holds a water pot in her upraised left hand, the attribute in her right hand is not clear.

# 5

## *CONCLUSION*

In the foregoing pages it has been observed that Gopeshwar has witnessed art activities from time immemorial. Nature has provided adequate natural resources to this region as may be seen in the vast stretch of agricultural land surrounded by thick forests. These forests captured sufficient rain water which recharged the underground natural reservoirs resulting in perennial discharge of water in the form of natural springs and rivulets, thus catering to the potable and agricultural needs of the settlers.

Already in the sixth century AD, it must have produced sufficient social surplus so as to maintain a religious establishment of considerable importance, which inspired the Nāga community to set up an iron trident here in subsequently as is evident from inscriptional, sculptural and literary sources.

The *Kedārkhaṇḍa*, one of the local *purāṇas*, while giving a detailed description of the holy places of Garhwal region, adds a dialogue between Pārvatī and Śiva. During the course of this dialogue Lord Siva narrates the importance of Gopeshwar to Goddess Pārvatī as follow:-

To the west (of *Agnitīrtha*) is (the place) known by the name *Gosthalaka*. O Devī, there, along with you I dwell forever. (Here) is the (temple) known by the name Paśvīśvara, which increases devotees' love (for me). There (stands) my trident, an amazing symbol. (If one) moves it with bodily vigour it does not shake. (However, if one) merely touches it by (ones) little finger with devotion it shakes repeatedly. O queen of gods, look, (there are) other symbols there. There is a tree which is ever-flowering (even during) odd time (he who murmurs) prayers for five (consecutive) nights intensely, he attains such supreme felicity as is difficult to be accomplished even by the gods. (He who) dies here, dwells in my world. (He who has) murdered a Brahmin, (who is) a spirit-drinker, (or) even (he who has indulged) in amorous enjoyment with his preceptor's wife goes (to my world), O queen of gods, what to talk of (the like) others (*Kedarkhaṇḍa*, 55.7-13, translation by MP Joshi).

Art remains scattered in Gopeshwar stand testimony to the religious importance of this place as already noted above.

The available archaeological evidence suggests that sometime before seventh century AD Uttarakhand experienced a devastating earthquake of very high magnitude resulting in complete destruction of several temples. This accounts for the presence of early images *vis-a-vis* total disappearance of the temples in which these images were set up (Joshi 2011b). As may be seen, the archaeology of Gopeshwar lends remarkable support to this view.

Thus, Gopeshwar offers a challenging field to studies relating to past society, environment, economy, art and architecture of Uttarakhand. This is the only site where one can study the art of Uttarakhand from its genesis through florescence, to ultimately its decline and downfall.

It is worthwhile to note that there are several scholars (Singh 1986; Nautiyal 1969; Śivaramaṃurti 1974) who suggest that some sculptural representations found in Uttarakhand represent the art of the Pratihāras. Joshi (1989a) has questioned this suggestion. Therefore, a fresh appraisal of the art of Uttarakhand is called for.

# SELECT BIBLIOGRAPHY

*Annual Report on Indian Epigraphy 1966-67*, Archaeological Survey of India, pp. 45.

*Annual Report on Indian Epigraphy 1968-69*, Archaeological Survey of India, pp. 58.

Agarwala, V.S. 1965. "*Studies in Indian Art*", Vishwavidyalaya Prakashan, Varanasi.

Atkinson, Edwin T, "*The Himalayan Gazetteer or The Himalayan Districts of the North Western Province of India*". Low Price Publications, Delhi.VL- I pp. 467- 68, & VL- II pp 511-12.

Banerjea, J.N, 1956. "*The Development of Hindu Iconography*", II ed. University of Calcutta, Calcutta.

Bhatt R C, Kenneth L Kvamme, Vinod Noutiyal, K. P. Noutiyal, Sanjeev Juyal and Sudhi Chand Noutiyal 2008-2009. "Archaeological and geophysical investigation on high mountain cave burial in Uttarakhand Himayala India". *Studies in South Asian Art and Architecture*. 30, 1-16.

Buhler, G. 1892 "The Prashasti of the temple of Lakhamandal" at Madha in Jounsar Babar- Vol. I *Epigraphica Indica*, pp.10-15.

Chhabra, CH.(1953-54) "Devprayag Brahmini inscription", *Epigraphica Indica* Vol XXX, Archaeological Survey of India pp.133-35.

Carnac, H Rivett. 1877. "Rough notes on some ancient sculpturings on rocks in Kumaon,similar to those found on monoliths and rocks in Europe." *Journal of the Asiatic Society of Bengal*, XLVI (I) : pp.1-15.

Dabral, Śivaprasad. 2028V.S. *Uttarakhanda ka Rajanaitika tatha samskritika itihasa*, Bhaga 4, *Gadhavala ka Itihasa*, I.Viragatha-prakasana, Dogada, Garhawal.

*Indian Archaeology -A Review (1953-54)*, pp. 11-12.

*Indian Archaeology -A Review (1971-72),* pp. 80.

Indraji Bhagwanlal. 1881 "An inscription at Gaya dated in the year 1813 of Buddha's nirvana, with two others of the same period, *The Indian Antiquary*", A journal or oriental research Vol. X, Swati Publication, Delhi.pp.345.

Joshi, Maheshwar. P.2011. Uttarakhand Himalaya ke Dasa-Silpakara: Adya praudyogiki evam adya bauddhika chimtana ke sampadaka. In: C.L. Pradyot et al (eds), *Uttarakhand ke Silpakara: Eka Samagra Adhyayana*. In press.

2010. "On the origin of the neo Indo-Aryan Pahadi Language of Uttarakhand and Western Nepal Himalaya". *Lingua Posnaniensis*, LII (2):pp. 51-65.

2009a. "The riddle of Asoka Challa". In: Devangana Desai and Arundhati Banerji (eds.), *The Mirror of Indian Art, Essays in Memory of Shri Krishna Deva*: New Delhi: Aryan Books International. pp. 353-60.

2009b. "Advent of polities in Kumaon and Garhwal". In: Marie Lecomte-Tilouin (ed.), *Bards and Mediums: History, Culture and Politics in the Central Himalayan Kingdoms*:. Almora: Almora Book Depot.pp. 327-71

2007. "The Kunindas and the Katyūrīs vis-a-vis Pona Silavarman". In: S.P. Shukla, R.S. Bisht, M.P. Joshi and Prashant Srivastava (eds.), *History and Heritage*:Delhi: Agam Kala Prakashān. pp.309-15

2005. "Kumaon and Garhwal: State and society". In: J.S. Grewal (ed.), *The State and Society in Medieval India*: New Delhi: OxfordUniversity Press. pp. 292-312

1995. "Art of Uttaranchal: an introduction". In: Maheshwar P. Joshi and Lalit Prabha Joshi (eds), *Rishi, II: Almora*: Shree Almora Book Depot. Pp. 95-118

1989. "Morphogenesis of Kuninda: A Numismatic Overview", Shree Almora Book Depot. pp. 100-101

1989. "Katyūrī art (cir. 650-1200 A.D.): an introduction". *Bulletin of Museums and Archaeology in U.P.*, pp. 43-44: 17-28.

1988. "Early burial practices in Kumaon: some recent discoveries". *Bulletin of Museums and Archaeology in U.P.*, pp. 41-42: 23-30.

1987. "Dots, cup-marks and pits vis-a-vis the megaliths: new evidences from Kumaon". *Puratattva*, pp. 16: 25-28.

1986b. "Śiva the Auspicious as depicted in some Kumaoni sculptures". In: Lokesh Chandra et al (eds.), *Dimensions of Indian Art*: Delhi: Agam Kala Prakashan. pp.211-20.

1986a. "The Religious history of Uttarakhanda: sources and materials". In: L.P. Vidyarthi and Makhan Jha (eds.), *Ecology, Economy and Religion of Himalayas: (Proceedings of National Seminar)*, Delhi: Orient Publications. pp.193-216.

1981. "Lali: A unique sculpture from Kumaon". *East and West*, 31 (1-4): pp.131-32.

1980. "A newly discovered early image of Visnu". *East and West*, 30 (1-4): pp.97-98.

1970. "*Almora and Pithoragarh Temples: Their Architecture and Iconography*" (unpublished Ph.D. Dissertation), Lucknow University : Lucknow.

Joshi, M.C. 1970 "Metal sculptures in the Kumaun hills and the tradition about the Pona Raja" in *Journal of the Oriental Institute*, XIX, 4: 433-39.

Kathoch, Yasavant Singh, 1981. "*Madhya Hiamalaya ka Puratattva*", the Author, Lucknow, pp.48-81.

1996 Madhya Himalaya, Part-I, "*Sanskriti ke padhchinha*", Bhagirathi Prakashan, Tehri Garhwal pp.82-87.

2003 "*Madhya Himalaya ki Kala (Ek Vastushastrya Adhhayan)*", Part-II, Vinsar Publishing Company, Dehradun. pp.115-204.

Khanduri, B.M.1994, "*Archaeology of Alaknanda Valley* (Central Himalaya)", Book Indian Publishing Co. New Delhi. pp. 16-30.

Khanduri, B.M. and P.M. Saklani 2003 "Central Himalaya (Bibliographic Reference on Archaeology)", *Culture and History*, Srinagar Garhwal, pp.8-10.

Kielhorn, F. 1896, *Indian Antiquary*, A journal of oriental research Vol. XXV, Swati Publication, Delhi. pp. 177-184.

Kedar Khand, 2007 translated by Pandit Sh. Brijratna Bhatacharya, Choukhamba Sanskrit Pratishthan, Delhi pp. 282-283.

Mathpal, Yasodhar. 1987. "Uttarakhanda mem sanskriti ka pragaitihasika prishthabhumi", *Uttarakhand, 1: 1-8*. Edited and published by Pramod Joshi for Uttarakhand Shodh Sansthan, Pant Nagar.

Nautiyal, K.P. 1969. "*The Archaeology of Kumaon, including Dehradun*", Chowkhamba Prakashan, Varanasi.

Nautiyal, K.P. and B.M. Khanduri 1986, "New cultural dimension in the Central Himalayan region of Uttarakhand". An Archaeological assessment Annali. 66: pp.77-100.

Powell Price, J.C. 1930 "Some notes on the Early History of Kumaon" in *Journal of the U.P. Historical Society*, IV,ii pp.5-14.

Saklani, Atul. 1983. "Gvarakhyavadyara (grama Dumgri) ke sailachitra", Pahar, 1: 217-18 Edited and published by Sekhar Pathak for *Pahar*, Nainital.

Sadhu Ram. 1950, "Ancient temple and inscription of Palethi", (Tehri Garwhal), *Siddhbharthi*, V.V.R. Institute, Hosiyarpur, 2; pp. 273-277.

Singh, Sheo Bahadur. 1986. "The Uttarakhand art-some special features". In : Kalyan Kumar Ganguli and S.S. Biswas (eds.) *Rupanjali*, in Memory of O.C. Gangoly : 95-97, O.C. Gangoly Memorial Society, Calcutta.

Śivarammurti, C. 1974, "*Natraja in Art, Thought and Litrature*", National Museum, New Delhi.

Sarcar, D.C. 1955-56, *Epigraphica Indica* Vol.XXXI, Archaeological Survey of India, New Delhi-1987 pp. 277-298.

Tiwari, Rakesh. 1983. Sarvekshana, Report, 1980-81. (Gadhavala Kumaum Mandala), U.P. *Rajya Puratattva Samgathana*, Lucknow.

Traill, G.W. 1826, "Statistical Sketch of Kumaon" in *Asiatic Researches*, 16, pp. 137-234.

Vats, M.S. and V.S. Agarwala, 1944. "A note on sculptures at Lakhamandal". *Journal of the U.P. Historical Society*, XVII (i): pp. 87-94.

# Index

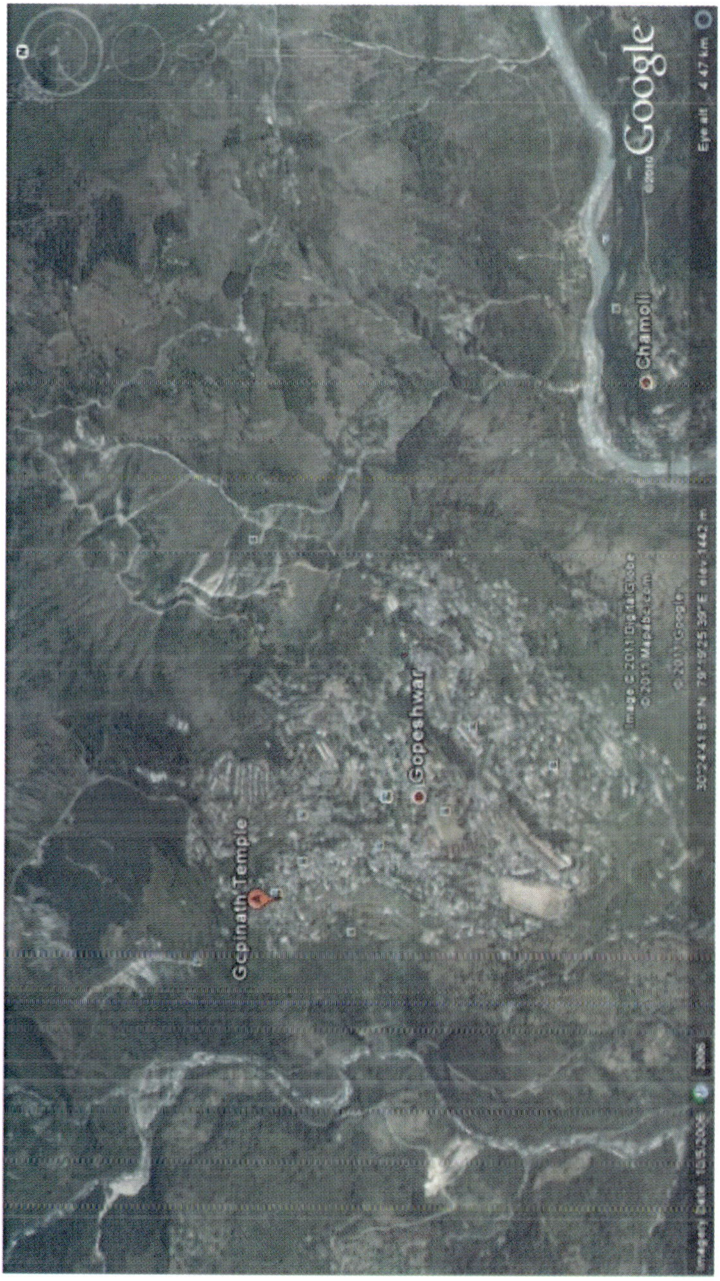


1. Satelite view of Gopeshwar

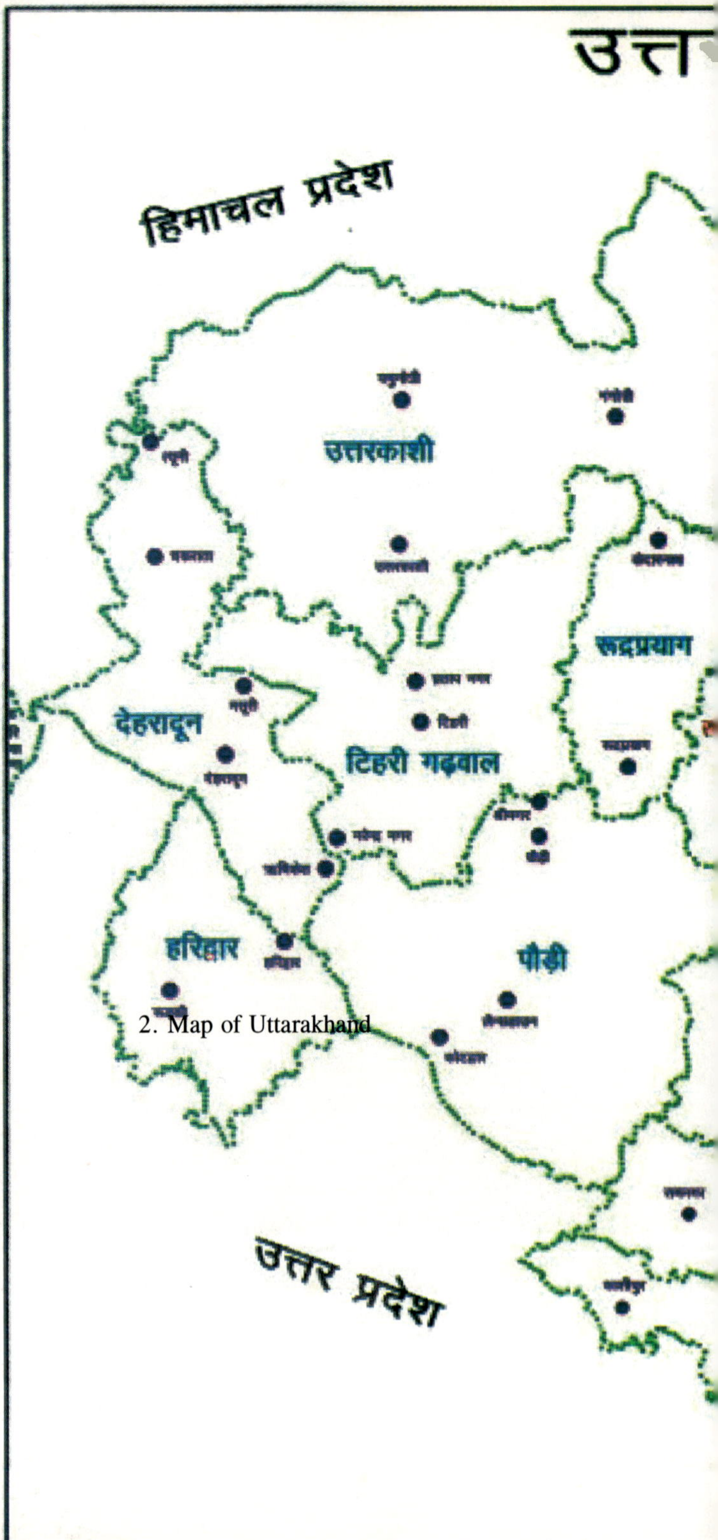


2. Map of Uttarakhand

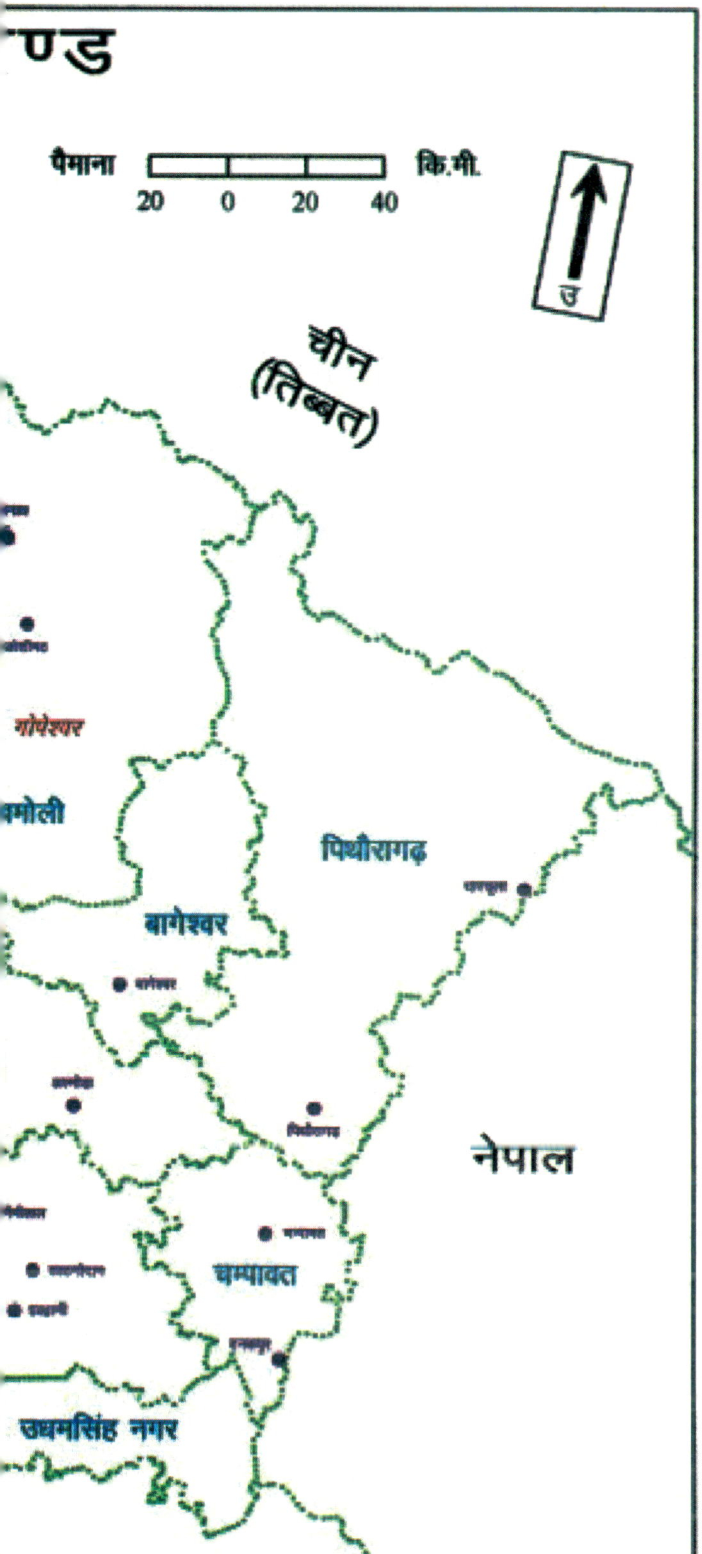

ण्ड
पैमाना
20 0 20 40
कि.मी.
उ
चीन
(तिब्बत)
गोपेश्वर
मोली
पिथौरागढ़
बागेश्वर
नेपाल
चम्पावत
उधमसिंह नगर

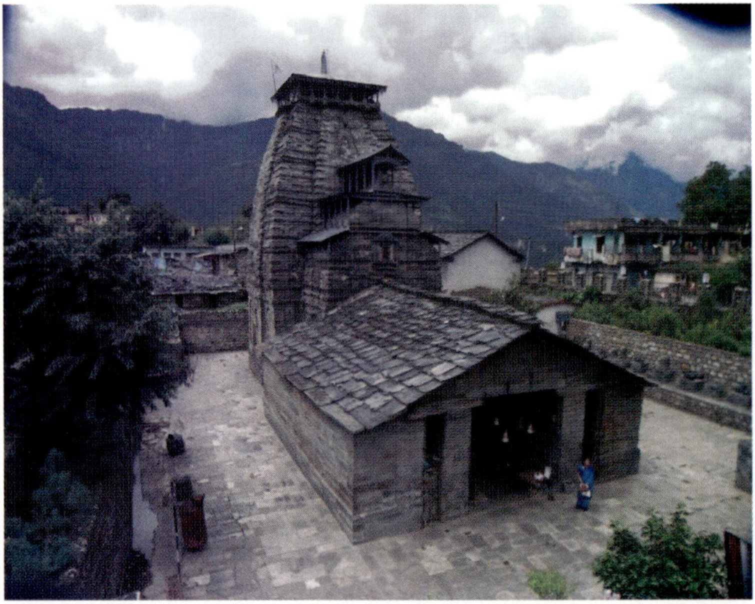

3. Śiva Temple

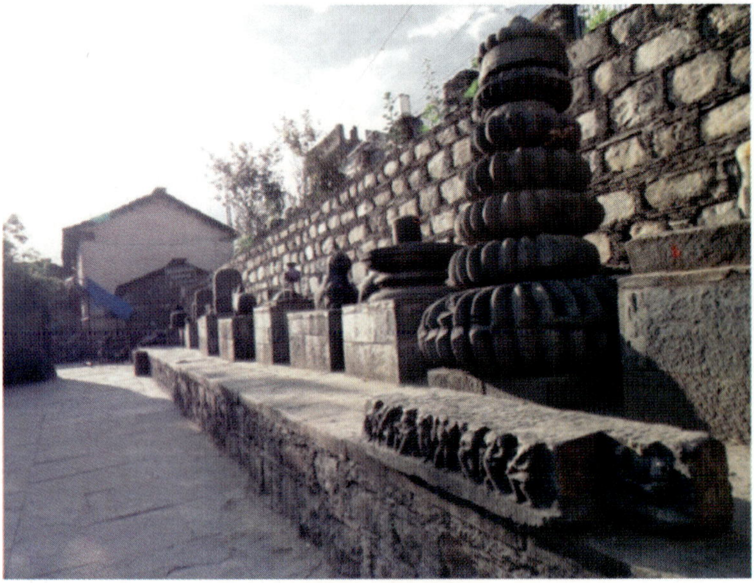

4. Amalakas

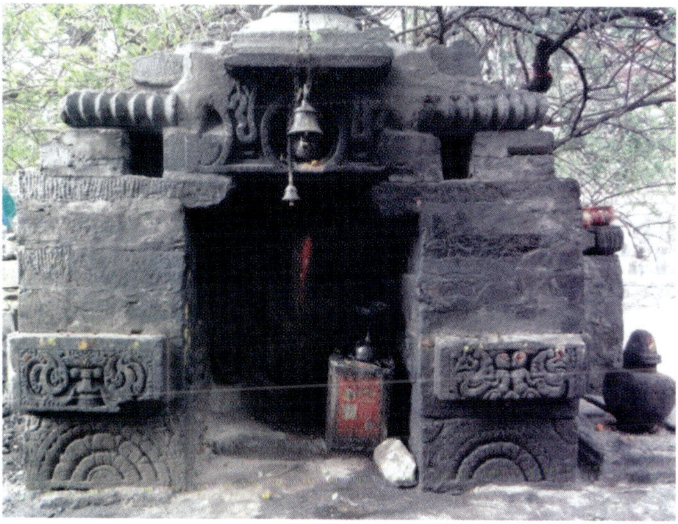

5. Ganesa Temple

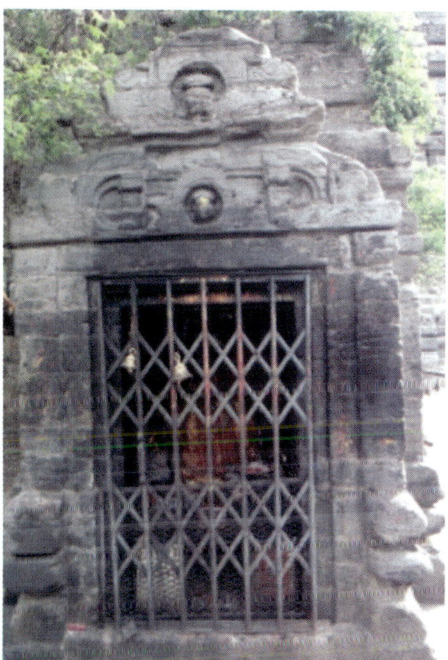

6. Mātā Mandir

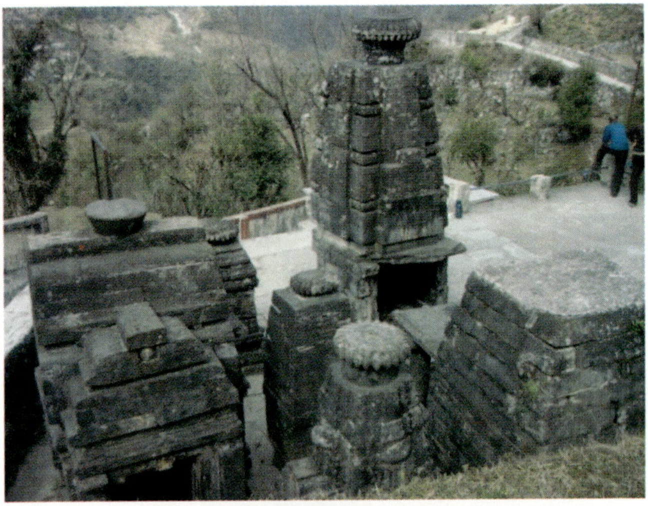

7, Group of Temples (Vaitarni)

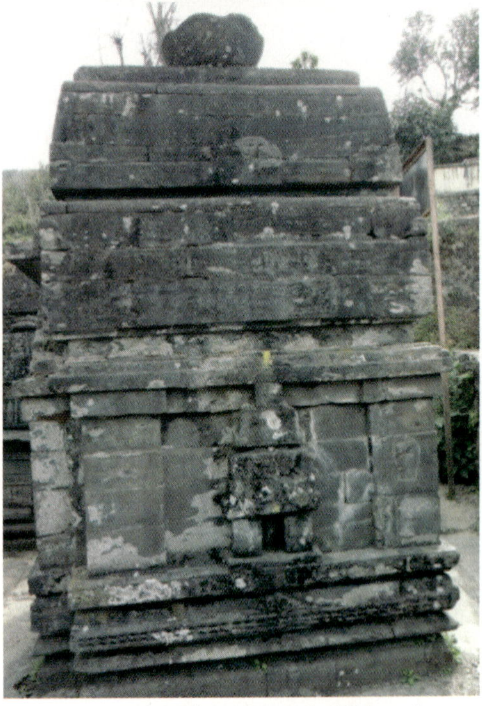

8. Vallabhi Sikhar Temple (Vaitarni)

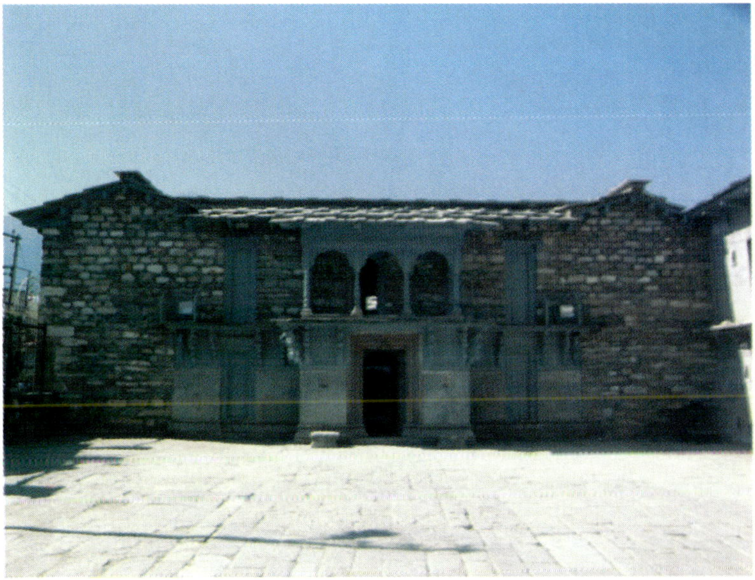

9. Rāwal Niwās

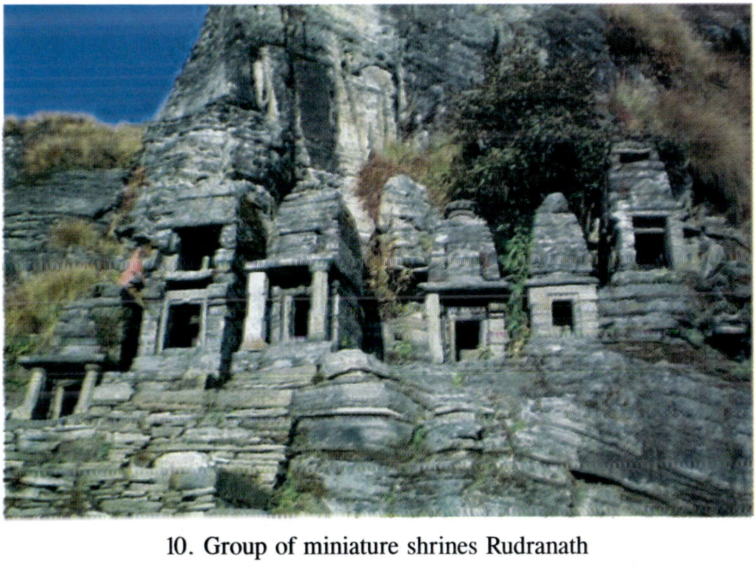

10. Group of miniature shrines Rudranath

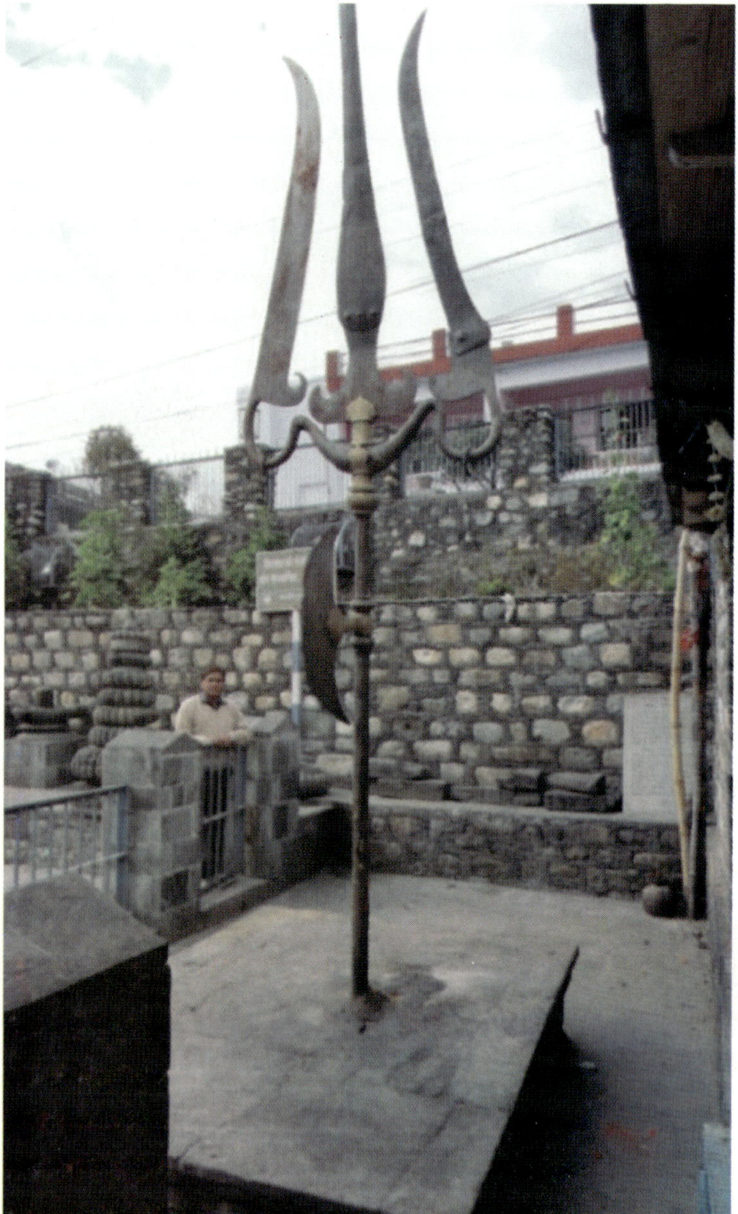

11. Iron trident

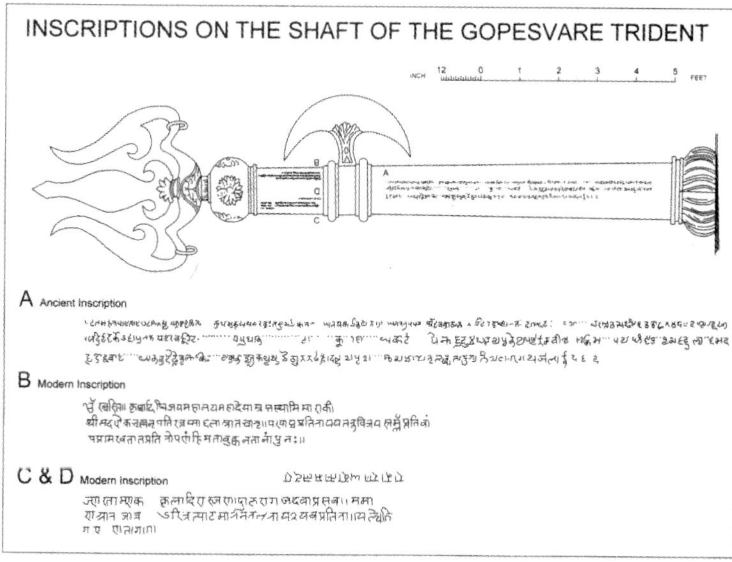


12. Inscribed trident

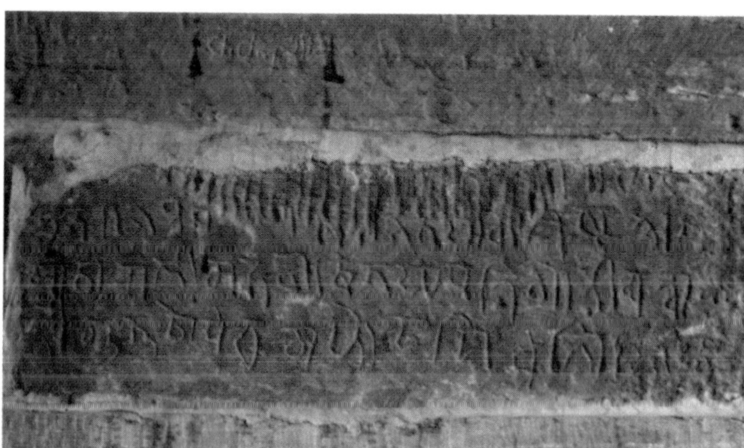

13. Inscribed stone slab of late period

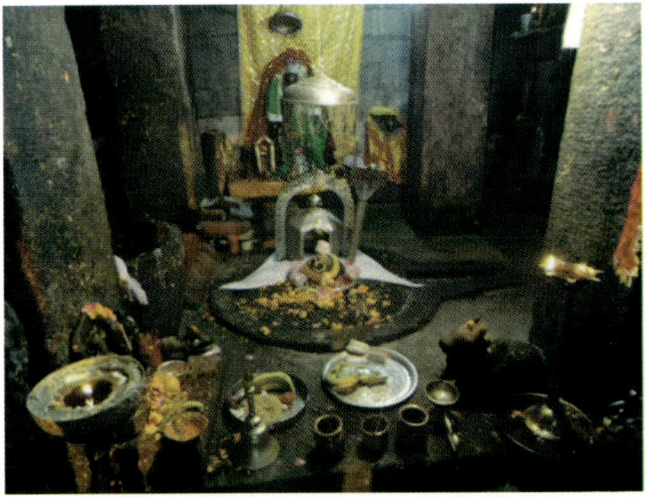

14. *Svayambhu Linga* in sanctum of main temple

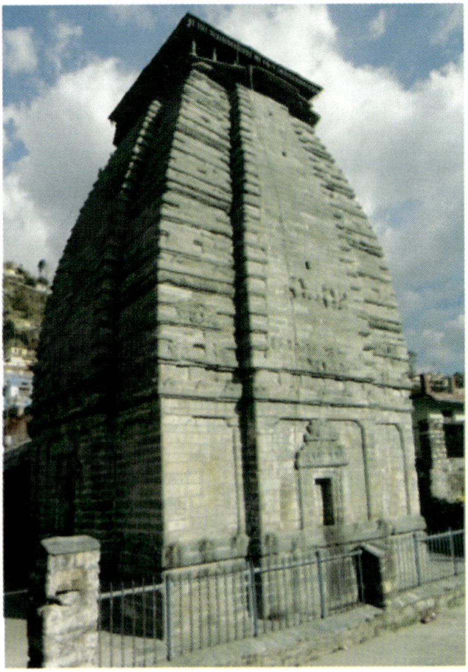

15. Triratha proliferation of main temple

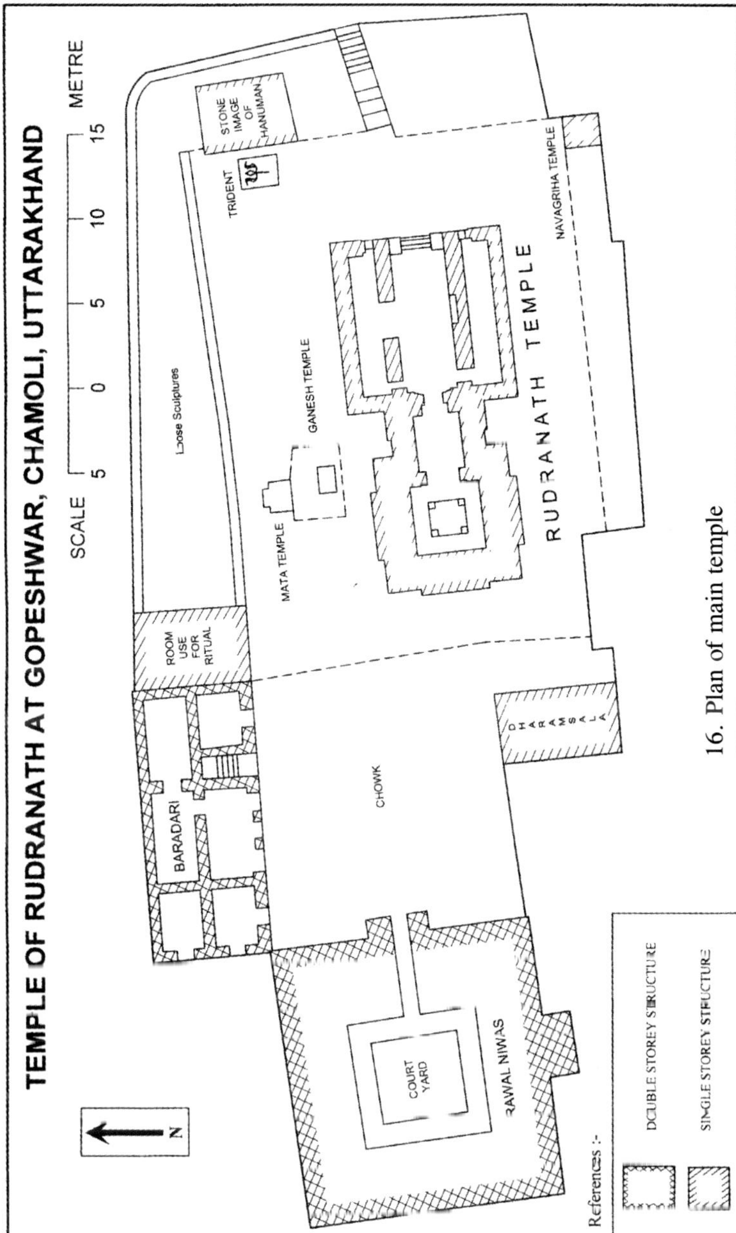


16. Plan of main temple

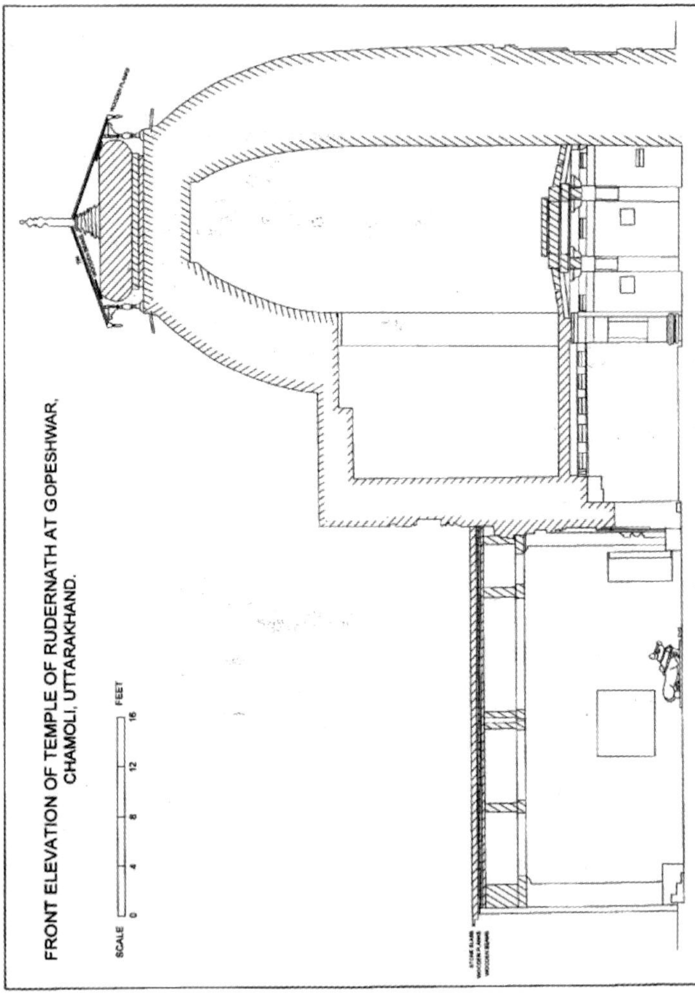


17. Main temple, front elevation

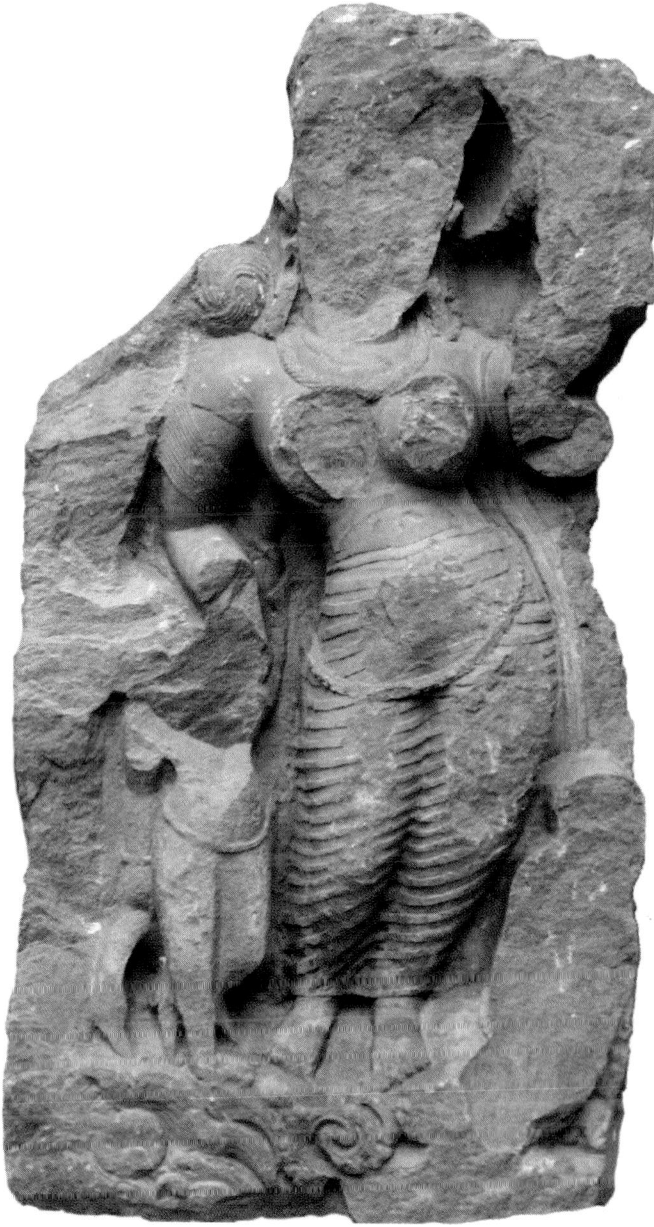

18. Goddess Ganga

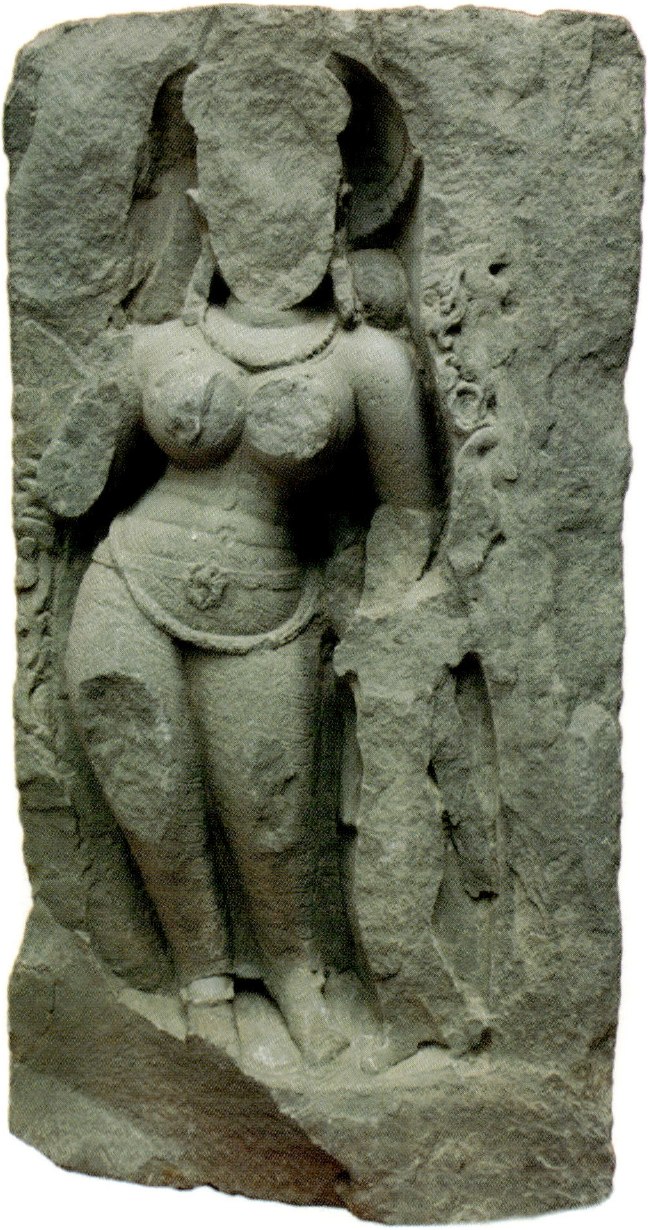

19. Goddess Yamuna

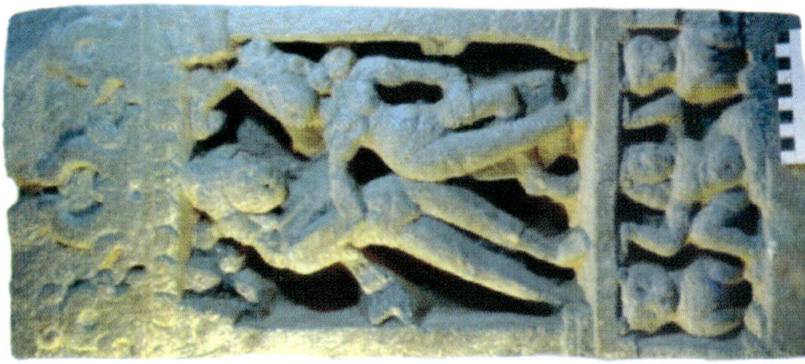

22. Mithuna figures

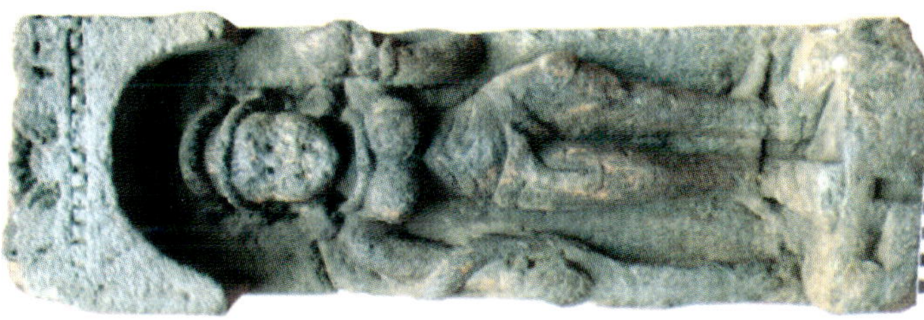

21. Yakshi

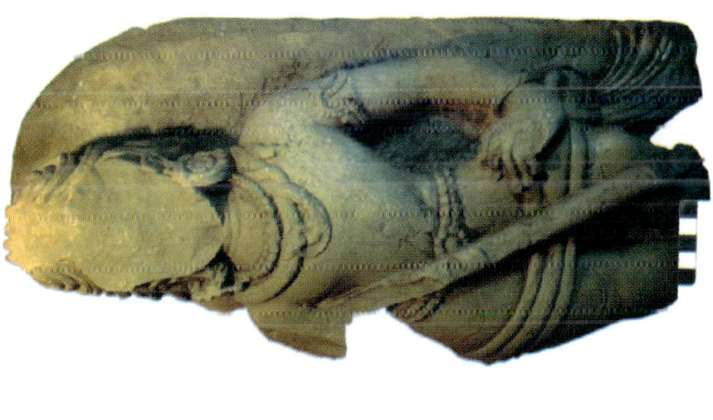

20. Shaivayat deity

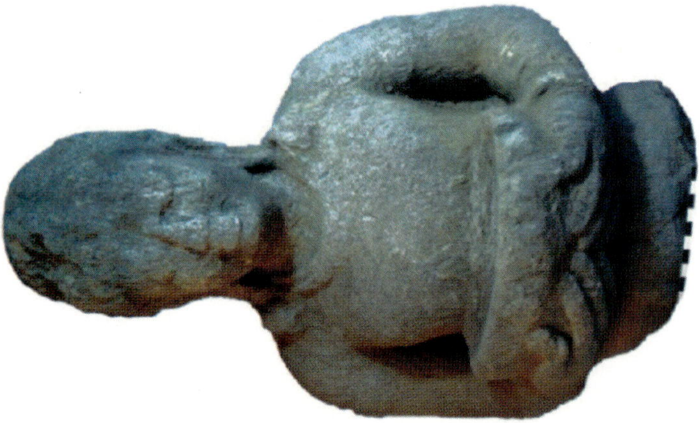

24. Male devotee

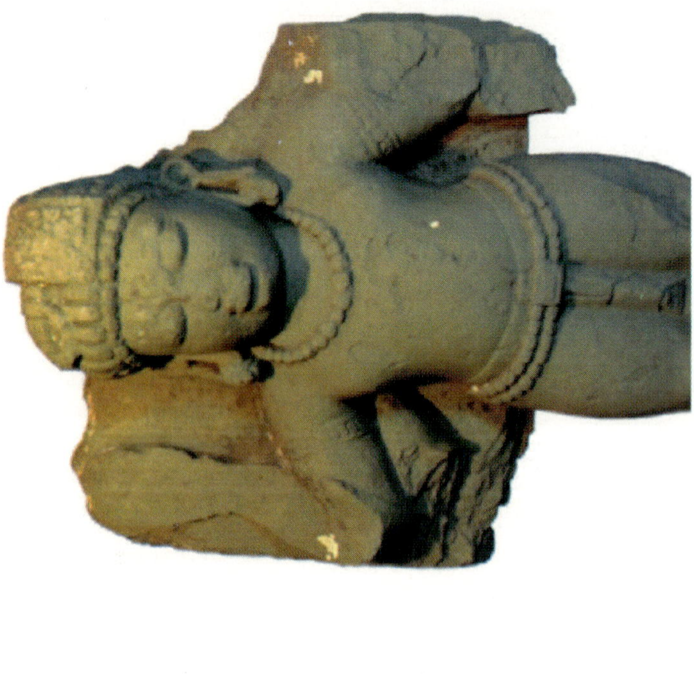

23. Harihara

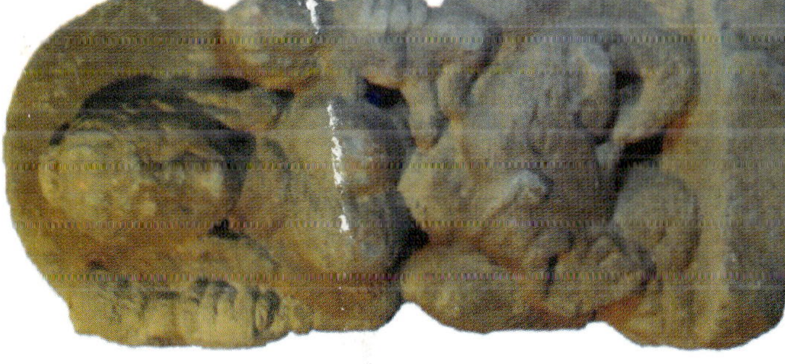

25. Indrānī

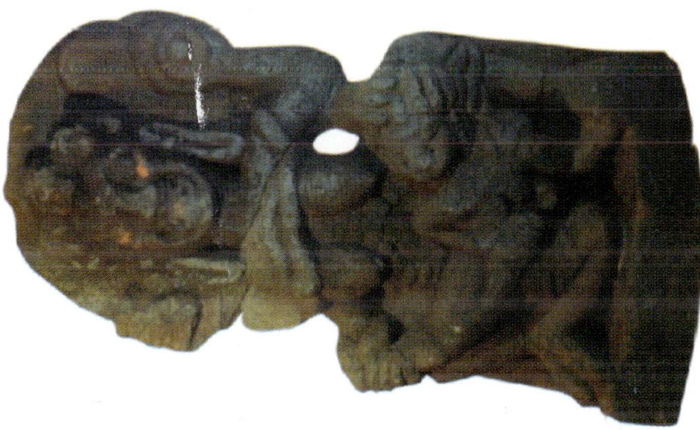

26. Chamuṇḍa

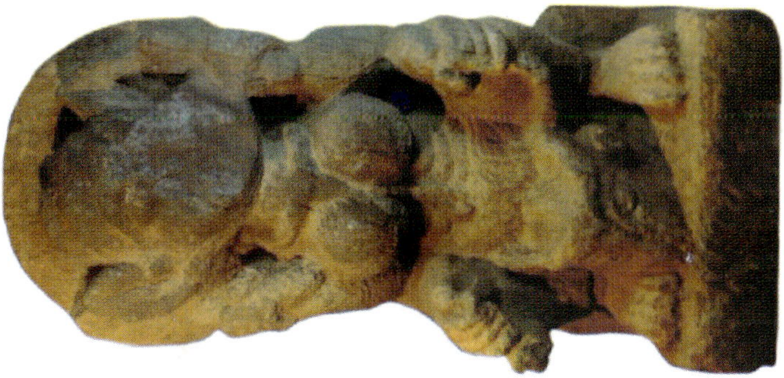

27. Vārāhi

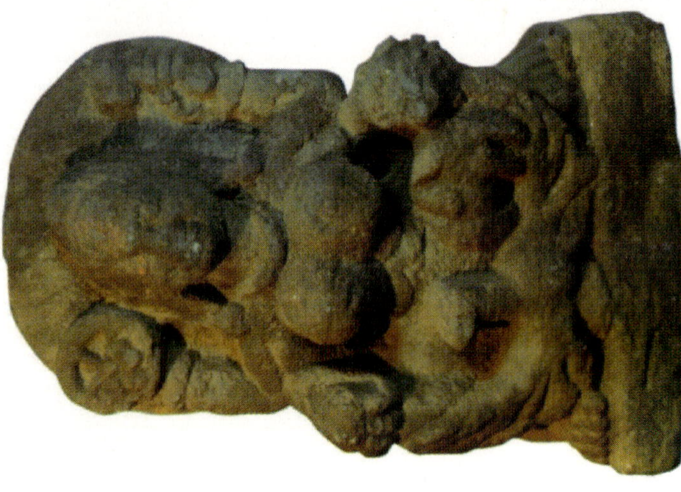

28. Vaishṇavi

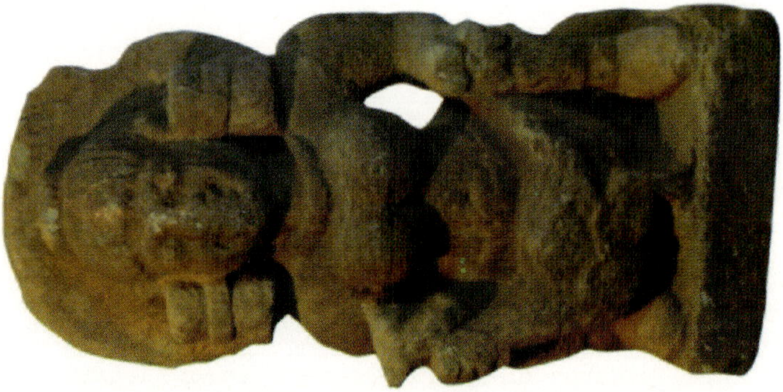

29. Kaumarī

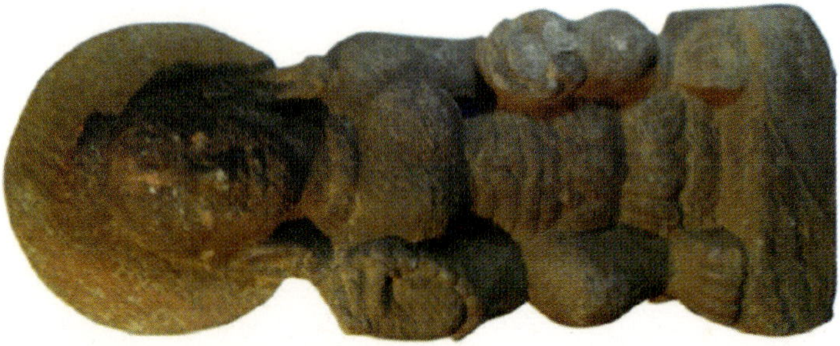

30. Brahāmaṇi

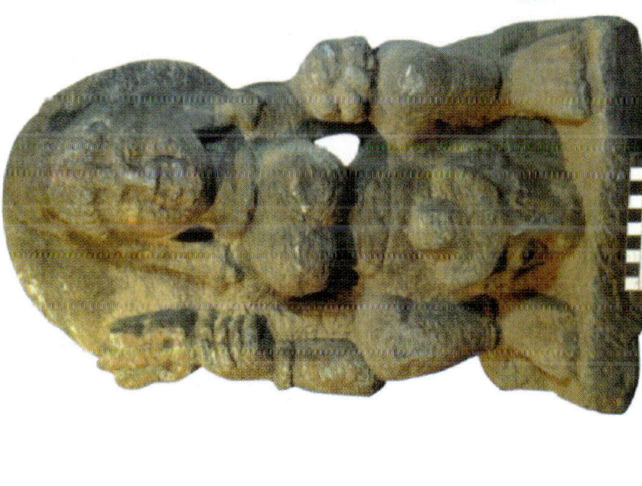

31. Maheshwari

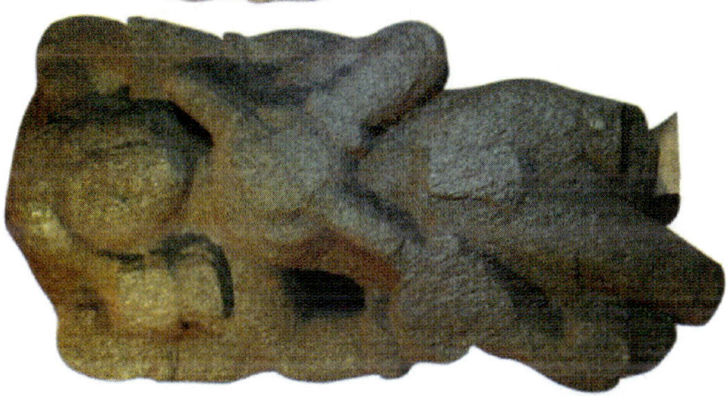

32. Virābhadra Śiva

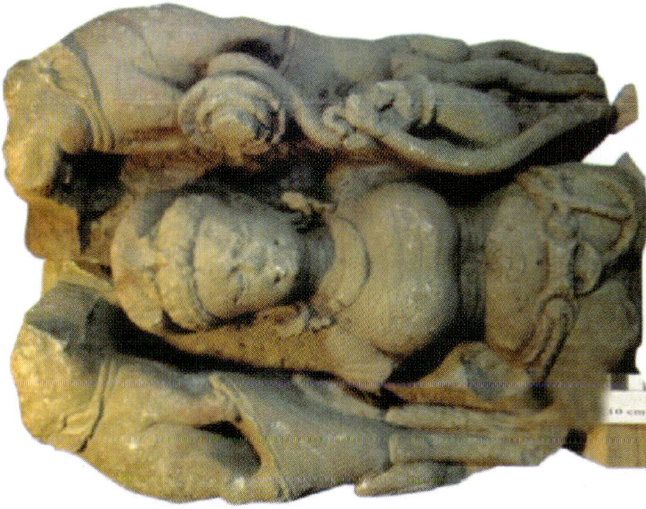

33. Gajalakshmi

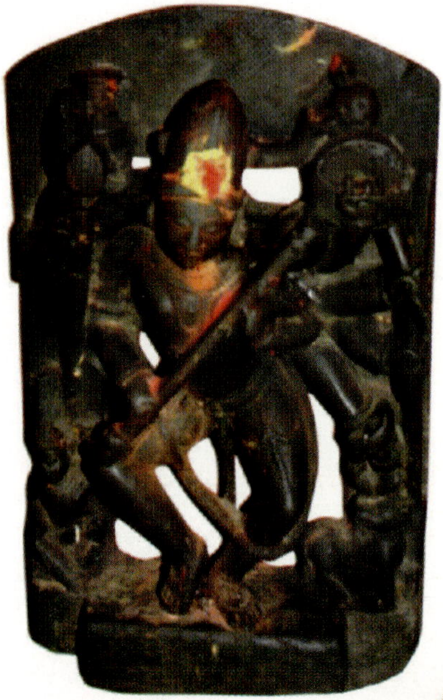

34. Nataraja Śiva

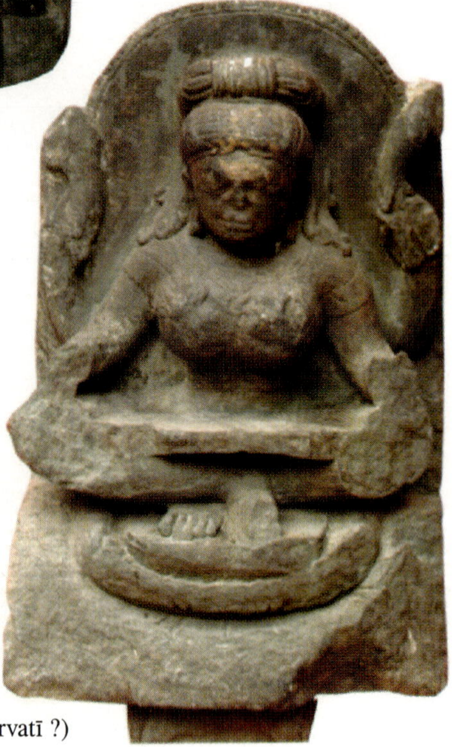

35. Female deity (Pārvatī ?)

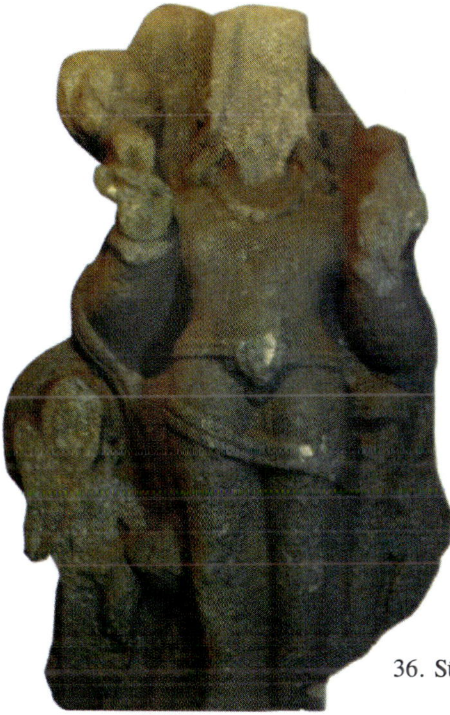

36. Sūrya

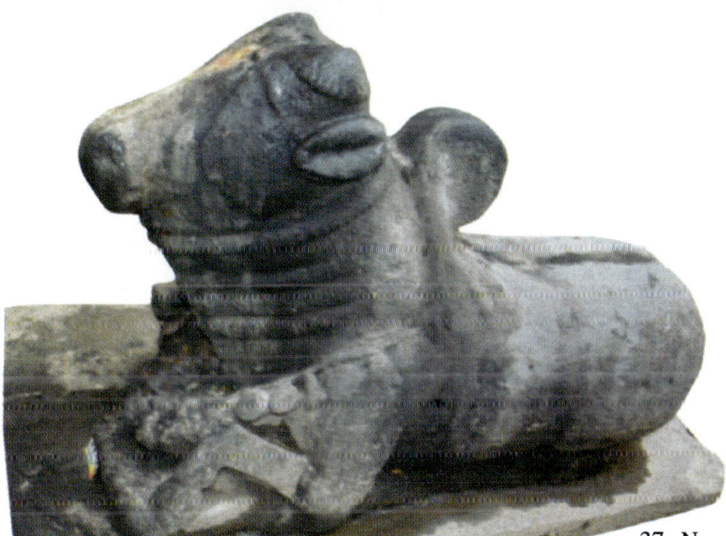

37. Nandi

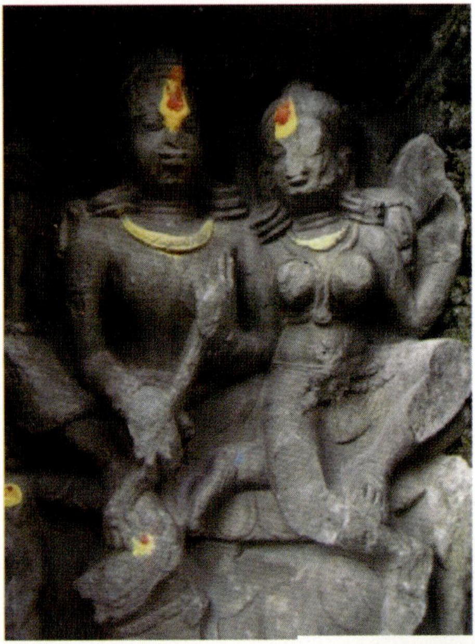

38. Umā-sahita – Vīnādhāramūrti

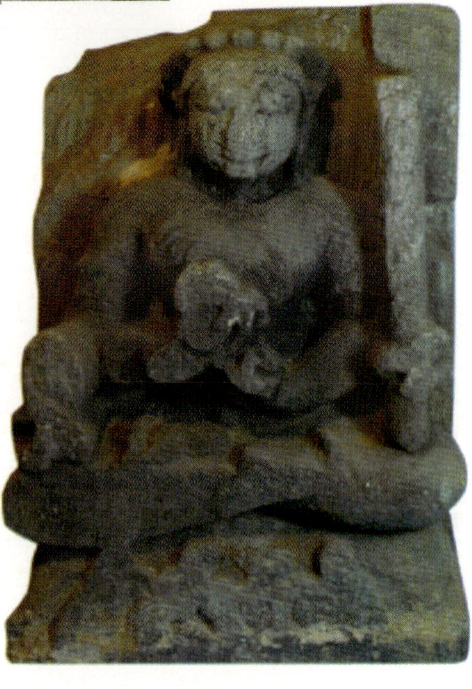

39. Lakulīsā

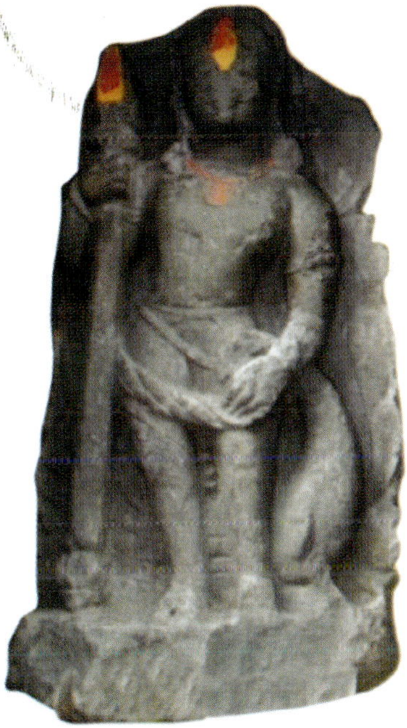

40. Kārtīkeya

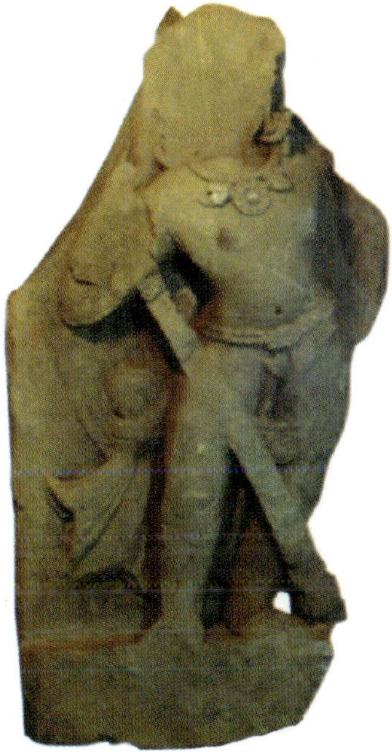

41. Kārtīkeya

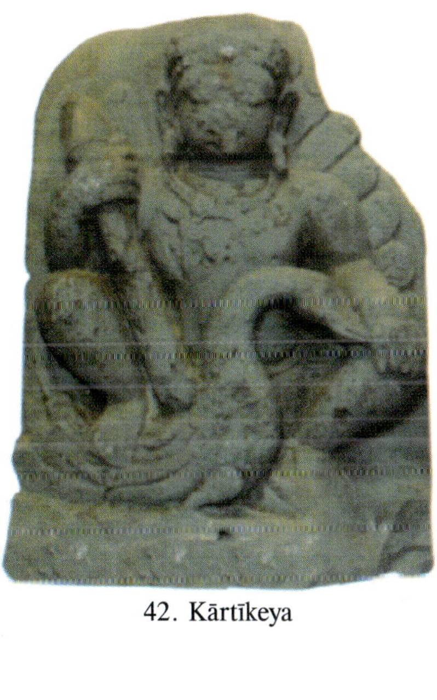

42. Kārtīkeya

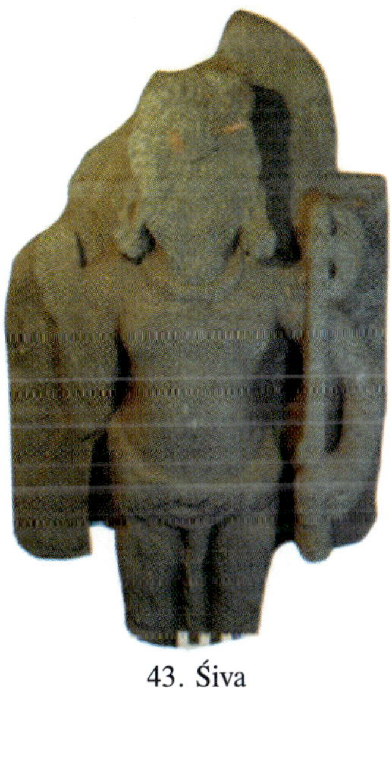

43. Śiva

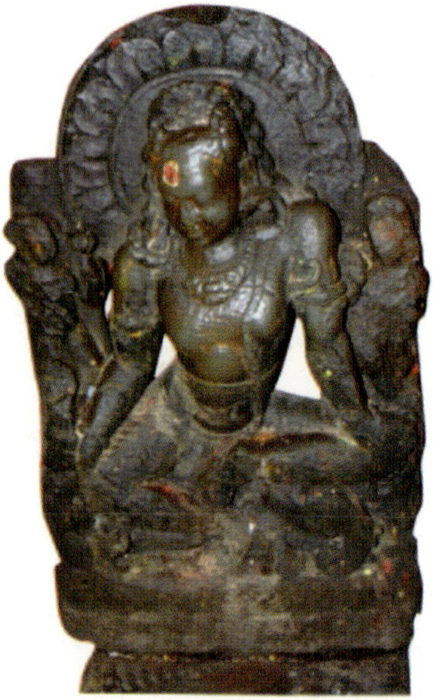

44. Indra

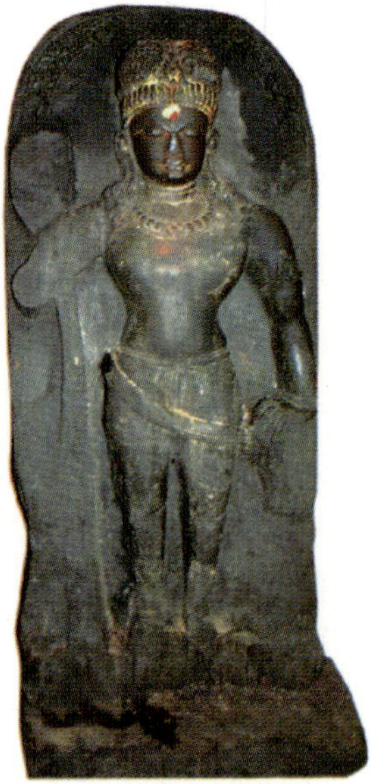

45. Śiva

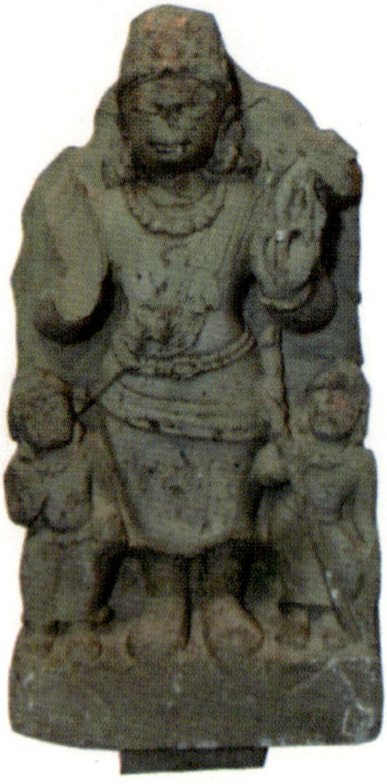

46. Sūrya

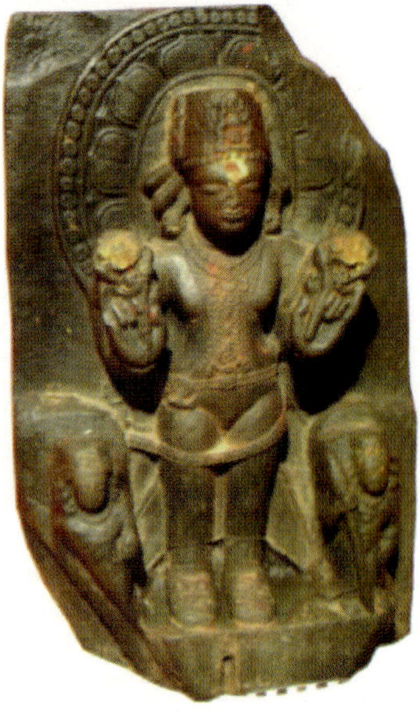

47. Sūrya

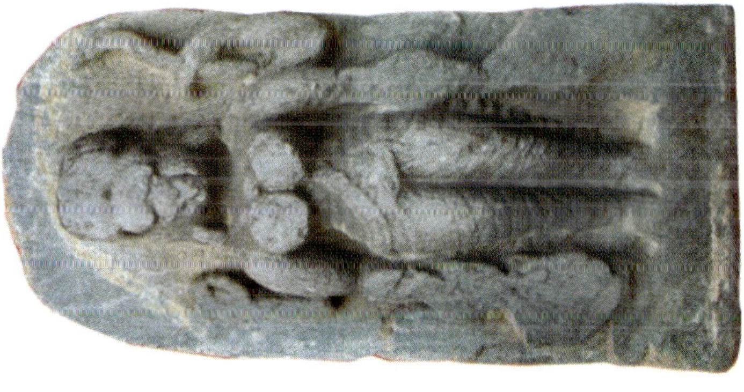

48. Pārvatī

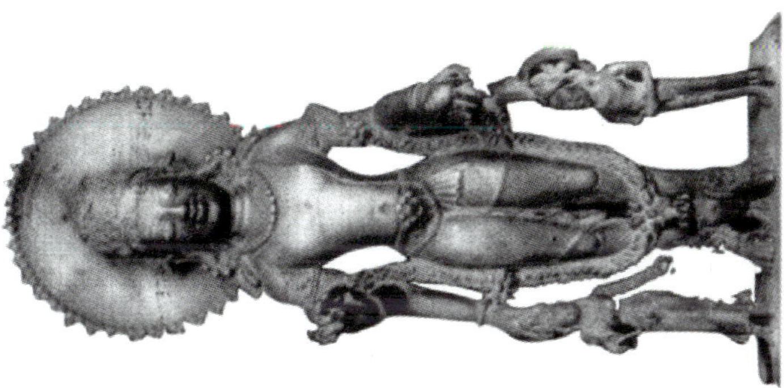

49. Vishṇu

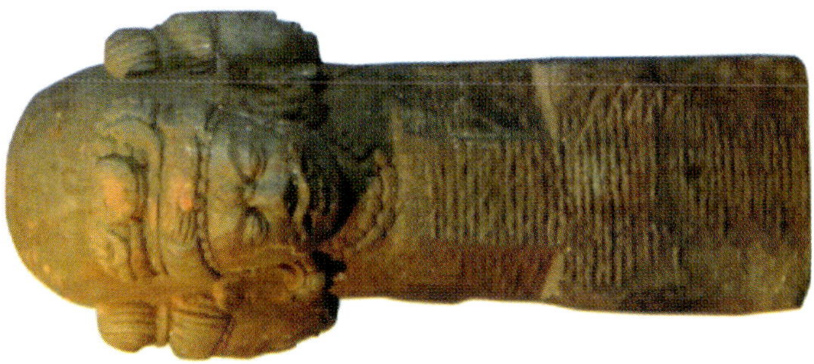

50. Chaturmukh Śiva-*linga*

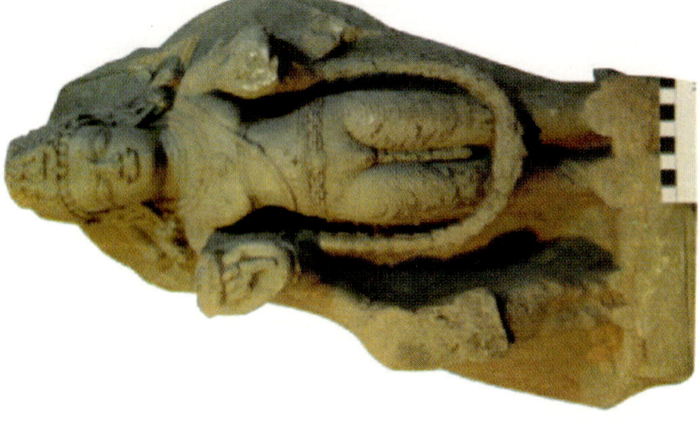

51. Vishṇu

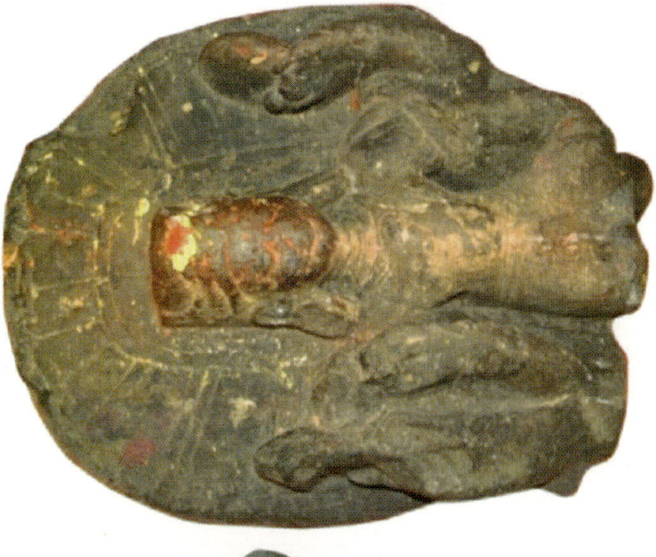

52. Vishṇu

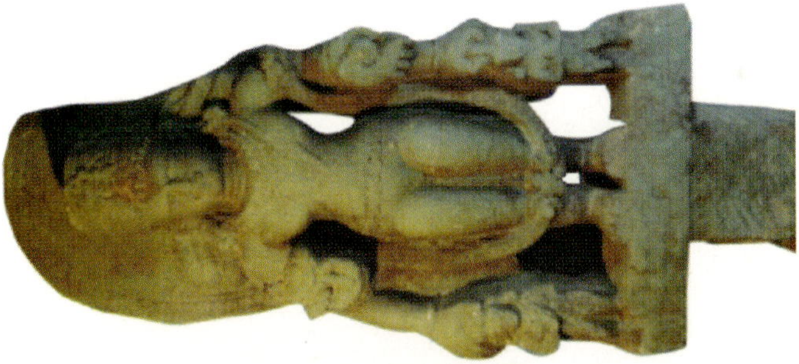

53. Vishṇu

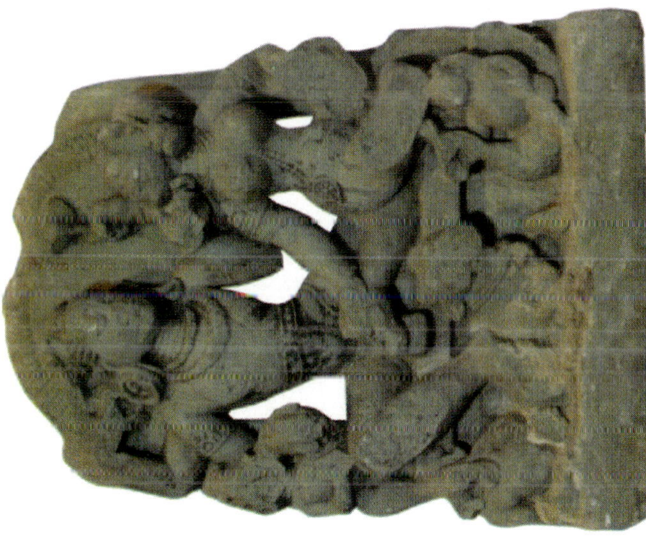

54. Umā-Maheśvara

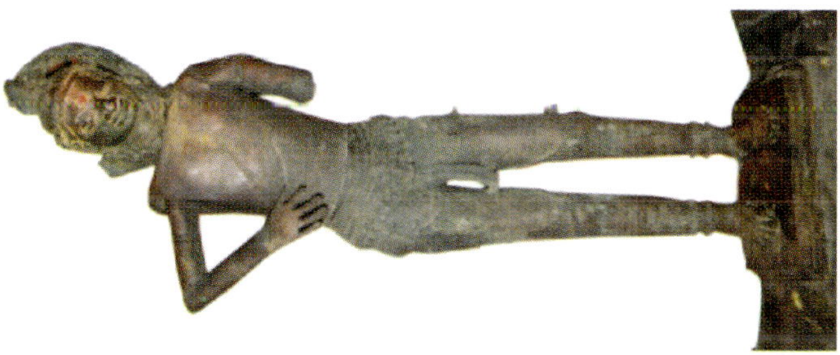

55. Metal deity

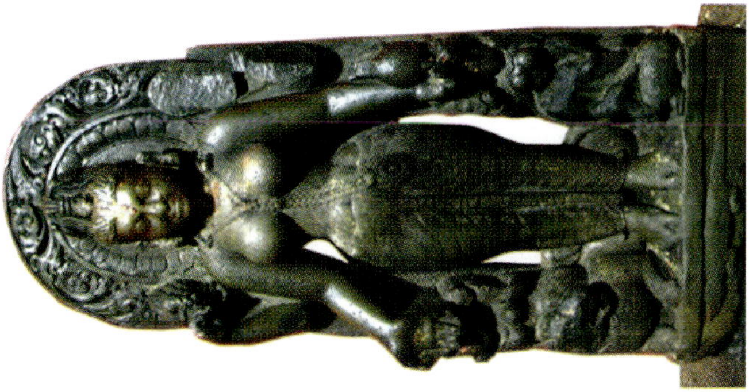

56. Pārvatī

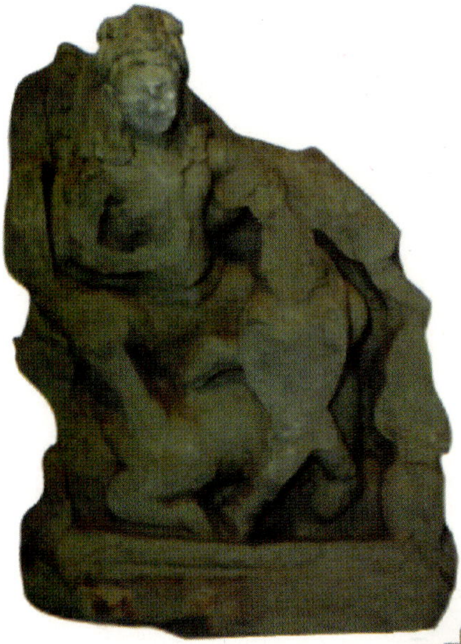

57. Umā-Maheśvara

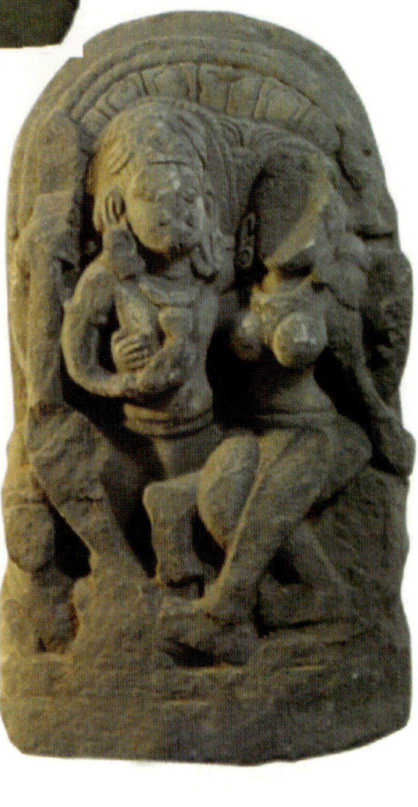

58. Umā-Maheśvara

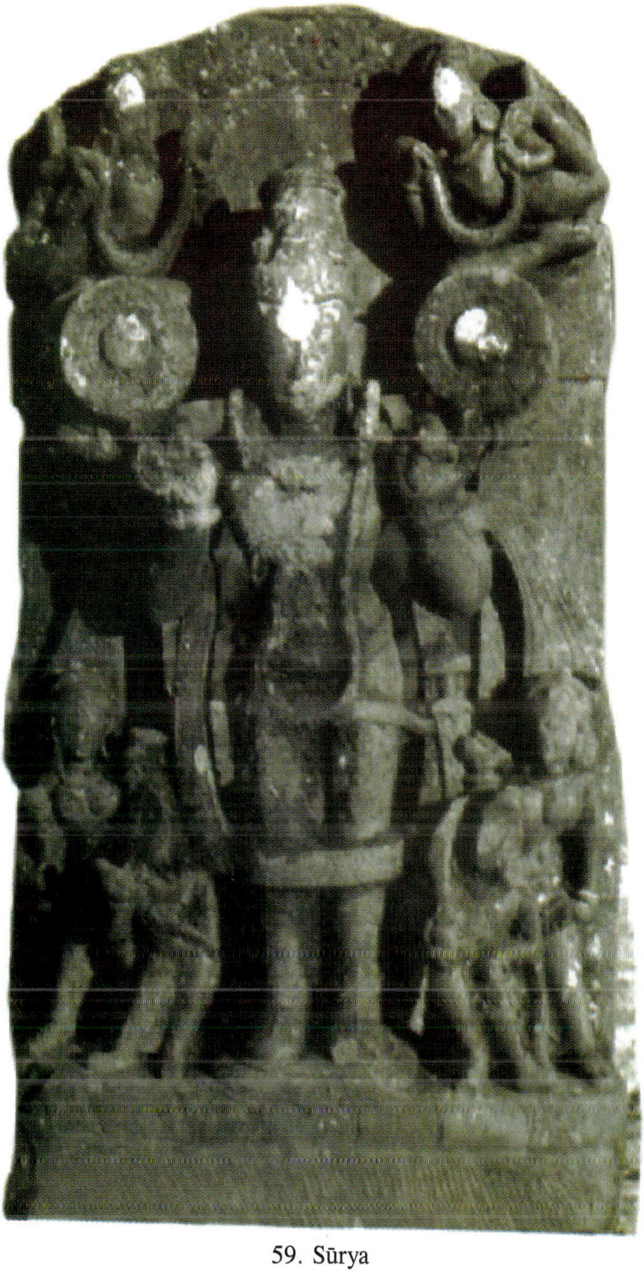

59. Sūrya

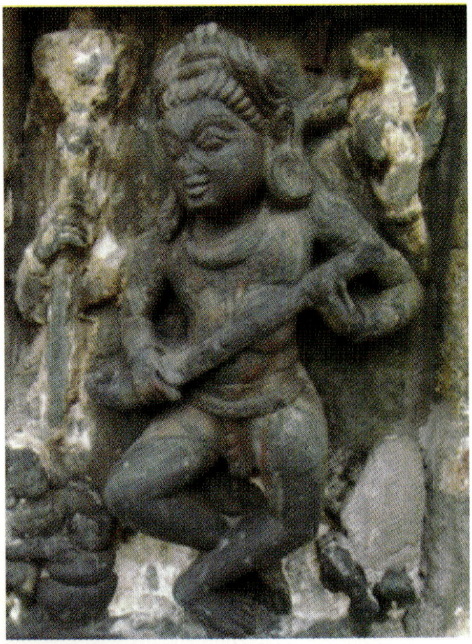

60. Viñādhara Śiva

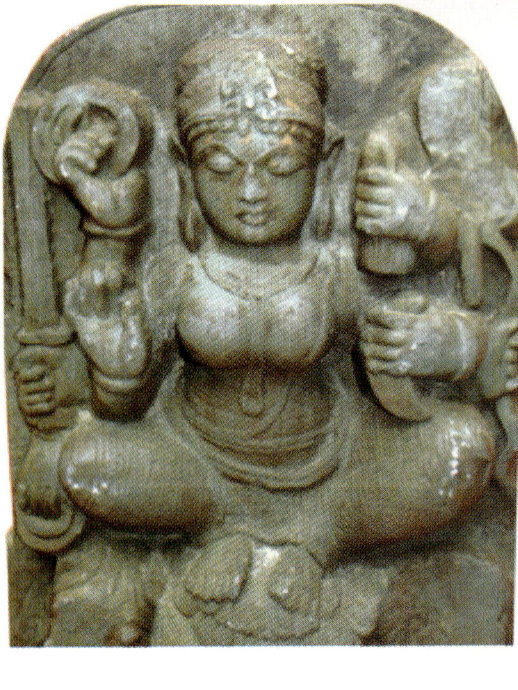

61. Durga

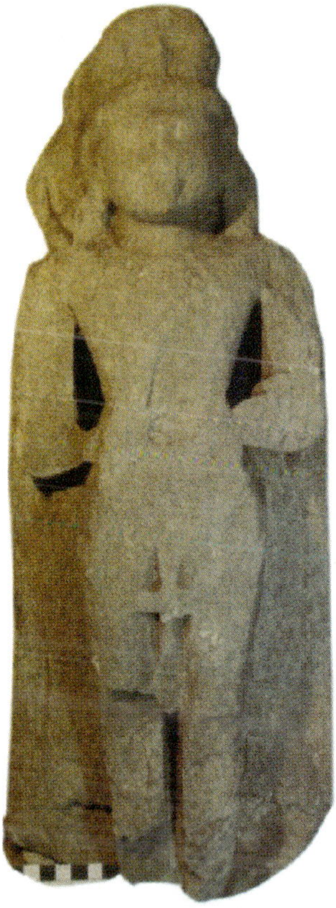

63. Standing male figure

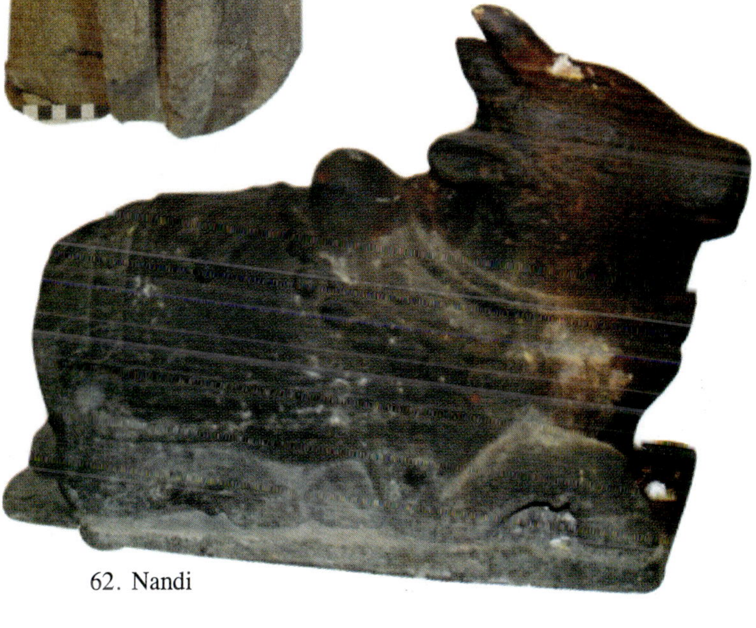

62. Nandi

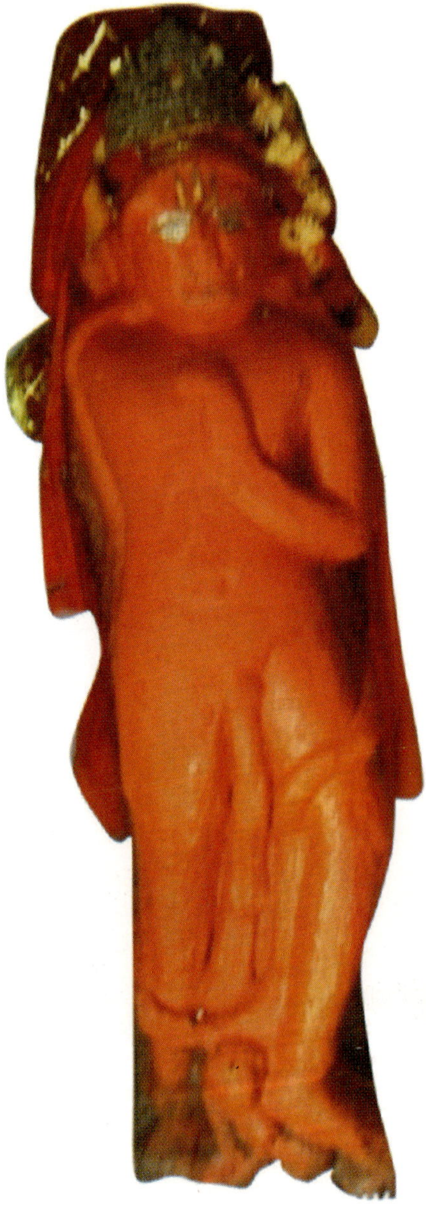

64. Standing male figure

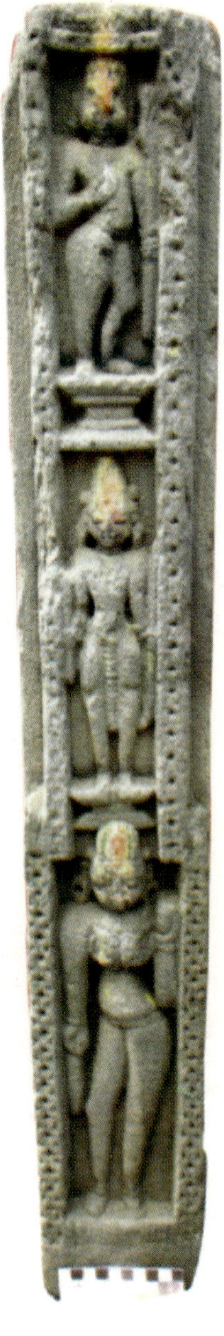

65. Dvārśakhā